CW00519968

Beyond Ourselves

A course which explores the wider meaning of our lives

Leader's Manual

Beyond Ourselves is Book 1 of *The God Who Is There,*
a discipleship course for small groups

by Roger Morgan

The Mathetes Trust

Copyright © Roger Morgan 2011
Second edition 2018

The right of Roger Morgan to be identified as the author of this work
has been asserted by him in accordance with the Copyright, Designs
and Patents Act 1988.

All rights reserved. No part of this publication may be reproduced,
stored in a retrieval system, or transmitted in any form or by any
means, electronic, mechanical, photocopying, recording or otherwise,
without the prior written permission of the copyright owner.

Design and layout by Alison Morgan.

Published by:
The Mathetes Trust
www.mathetestrust.org
Charity no. 1169869
ISBN 978-1-912124-11-4

Unless otherwise stated, all Bible translations are taken from the New
Revised Standard Version of the Bible, Anglicized edition, copyright ©
1989, 1995 by the Division of Christian Education of the National
Council of the Churches of Christ in the United States of America, and
are used by permission. All rights reserved.

All images reproduced by permission.

This course is edited by Roger Morgan. We are grateful to the following
people who contributed to the writing of the individual sessions: Anita
Benson, John Benson, Ian Bishop, Pete Greaves, Mike Harrison, Alison
Morgan, Richard Morgan, Michael Selman, Karin Silk, Elaine
Sutherland, Lauren Wicks, and Angela Zvespar.

.   Canon Roger Morgan is Director of The Mathetes Trust.

Beyond Ourselves

Contents

Preface

Welcome to the first book of our series on discipleship *The God Who is There*. Each book provides a course of ten sessions suitable for small groups. This book, *Beyond Ourselves,* asks the question 'Is there anything beyond ourselves?' or in other words 'Is God there?'. By the end of the course the course members should be able to say 'Yes – I am sure God is there, because I have experienced him for myself.' The second book, *The New Community,* is about continuing to find God to be there whenever a group of Christians meet and search for him together. The third book, *Shining Like Stars*, is about finding God to be there in ordinary day to day life.

The God Who is There takes its inspiration from *Rooted in Jesus*, a discipleship course written sixteen years ago for rural Africa. *Rooted in Jesus* has been highly successful, having been translated so far into 45 African languages and adopted in 16 countries. It has been used to transform many lives as well as whole churches and communities. Because of its success in Africa many people have asked us to release *Rooted in Jesus* for use in the West, believing, as we do, that discipleship is needed here too.

The God Who is There series is our response to that request. *The God Who is There* has the same aims and a similar style to *Rooted in Jesus*, and also has much overlapping content. At first we thought we could keep the same structure and chapter headings and just make a few revisions, but we found that this did not work and decided to do a complete rewrite. The illustrations and examples used in the two series have had to be very different because the issues and problems westerners face in their daily lives are mostly quite different from those people face in Africa. And in *The God Who is There* we have tried to relate to western moral and philosophical assumptions. For example, to most people in rural Africa it is obvious that God is there. But in the West to live by faith in God is to live in a way that stands out from the norm.

For each of the three courses in the series there is a Leader's Manual and an accompanying Coursebook for each group member. Books 2 and 3 also involve music, and come with a worship CD. The series is suitable for groups of any size. It will work well with just three people, but it could equally well be used by a large church with many groups meeting together at the same time.

The series was written by a team of contributors and edited by Roger Morgan, working in this first book with Anita Benson. The Mathetes Trust is able to offer training to churches or to group leaders using the course. If you would like to find out how we can support you, please do get in touch with us by emailing admin@mathetestrust.org or calling 01749 679865. Or visit our website, https://mathetestrust.org.

How the course works – notes for the leader

Beyond Ourselves envisages a group of between three and twenty people who will meet together for a series of ten sessions, each lasting an hour and a half. The session can be preceded by a shared meal or a simpler form of refreshment, or by a time of worship.

This book, the Leader's Manual, is for the leader only. It gives minute by minute suggestions for how to spend the time. You will need to prepare carefully and come up with your own detailed plan for each session. Some leaders will prefer to follow the book in every detail. Others may wish to adapt the course to suit their own style or to suit the composition of the group.

In each session the sections are carefully timed; you will need to keep your eye on the clock and stick more or less to these times. If you get behind on one section you should try to make it up on the next. With some groups this will be quite easy but with others, where people are more talkative, keeping to the timings will be more difficult. If this happens, you may wish to over-run a little, or you may prefer to complete one session in two meetings or even two sessions in three meetings. If you start the sessions late you are bound to run into problems. Better would be to start early and allow more time for the session.

Each session contains a key verse from the Bible for group members to write out on cards and keep with them. In the African version of the course, where it is normal for the groups to memorise the verses, our experience is that those who take the memorisation most seriously make the most progress. The same will be true for those who work through *The God Who is There* series. So suggest to the group that it would be a good plan for them to memorise these key verses. If they do decide to memorise they will benefit greatly from the experience, but if the group is opposed to the idea it is wise to go along with their wishes.

There is a separate member's coursebook which you should give to each of the group members during the first session. This coursebook contains exercises, four for each session, which are designed to help group members work out the practical implications of what they are learning. Three of the exercises follow on from the session, and one is there to help them prepare for the next session. There are various ways of introducing the exercises for groups of different kinds (see below), but do bear in mind that if the exercises are omitted, the impact of the course will be greatly reduced.

Here are three ways in which you could use the exercises:

- Agree with the group that each of them will choose one exercise and try to complete it before the next session starts. Those who are keen can do more than one. With most groups it will be best to work in this way. Make sure that time is allowed in the sessions to report back on the exercises.

- If your group lacks much formal education then it may work better if you choose one of the exercises for each session and suggest that you all tackle the same one. If reading skills are a problem it may be better to describe the chosen exercise orally and not use the coursebooks at all. Another idea which sometimes works well is for the group to divide themselves into pairs and then for each pair to meet up to do the chosen exercise together.

- As a third alternative you could choose to build the exercises into the group sessions themselves, and devote two meetings to each session. This will work extremely well if the group is happy to do the course over twenty sessions rather than ten.

There is more to leading a small group than just running meetings; a good leader will also care for the group members individually. So put time into developing a relationship with each group member. Do this in any way that seems appropriate, for example by meeting up for coffee, going shopping together, playing squash, doing something with your children, going to a film. If you show them that you love them, you will find that what you are teaching in the sessions will get across much more effectively.

Roger Morgan

Additional resources

If members of the group do decide to place their faith in Christ, you may find it helpful to give them a copy of *Decision: an explanation of what is involved in becoming a Christian.* *Decision* is a short and inexpensive booklet which summarises the steps on the road to faith and explains what to expect next. *Decision* is available from the Mathetes Trust website either singly or in packs of ten.

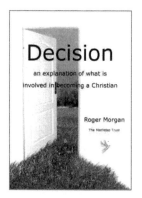

Decision

an explanation of what is
involved in becoming a Christian

Roger Morgan

The Mathetes Trust

Beyond Ourselves

Session 1: God, creation and me

Please note that this session is divided into 6 sections. Timings are given for each section, with 90 minutes in all. You may decide to leave some sections out, but if you want to include them all you will need to stick carefully to the timings. With most groups it will only rarely be sensible to end the sessions late. If at all possible start the session early; this will give you a bit more time and added flexibility.

Things you will need for this session :

- A whiteboard or flipchart
- Spare Bibles (in case anyone does not bring one)
- A large sheet of paper with Psalm 23.6 written out clearly, displayed in a prominent place in the room
- Small cards (small blank name-cards are available in stationers) for the memory verses – you will need a fresh supply every week
- Pens and paper for group members
- If you can, ask everyone to bring with them a picture of themselves as a baby; if you aren't able to ask them in advance make sure you have one of yourself.

Introduction   (15 mins)

Begin by introducing the course and the title *Beyond Ourselves.* Use your whiteboard or flipchart to write up the following questions.

- Is there anything beyond ourselves?

- Does reality consist of what we can see, touch and measure – or is there something more?

- If there is something more, what is it like, and how can we be in touch with it?

If this is a group which has met before, ask the members one by one to respond very briefly to the questions on the board.

If it is a new group, explain that these questions are what the course is all about, but that before you get down to looking at them together it would be good to start by getting to know one another. Ask each person to share their name and to explain briefly why they have joined the group.

Next give each person a Member's Coursebook. Turn to page 6 and point out that the coursebook begins with a summary of today's session. This summary is then followed by the key verse. Explain that for each session there will be a key verse which tries to capture the essence of what that session is about.

Then look at the exercise on page 7 of the coursebook. Research shows that 3 out of 4 people in the UK have had a spiritual experience of some kind. This means that if you are a typical group many of the group members will say 'yes' to some of the questions in the exercise. Ask them to look at the exercise and one by one make their response to the questions.

Do not allow this to lead to a long discussion, but move on within the allocated time. Before you move on explain briefly from your own personal experience why you yourself believe in God, and say that you hope that everyone in the group will have begun to share your experience before the course is over.

God the creator and designer of the Universe (15 mins)

Explain that during the course you will often look at the Bible together; make sure everyone has a copy. Explain that for you the Bible is like a map which enables you to navigate your way through life. How are we to make sense of the supernatural experiences we have just been discussing? Or more commonplace experiences like a family row, or an earthquake, or what's going on at a funeral? Say that in your experience the Bible sheds light on all these things.

Now ask the group to turn to **Romans 1.19-20**. Explain that this is the beginning of Paul's presentation of the Christian gospel which continues for the next 11 chapters of his letter to the Romans. Tell the group that the course begins where Paul began – with the creation of the universe. Read verses 19-20 aloud, and then summarise along the following lines:

Paul is saying that anyone who looks at the universe objectively can have no doubt that behind it lies a great Creator or designer, and that by looking at creation we can learn a great deal about the Creator himself. In our day Paul's view has been challenged by some scientists who argue that everything we see can be explained by chance and evolution. Other scientists dispute this, arguing that it is so improbable that the universe could have arisen by chance that there must be a designer behind it. They also say that while science helps us to understand how the universe has developed since it began, science will never be able to explain *why* it began. The fact that things exist at all is not a scientific issue but a philosophical or religious one.

Ask the group: "What are your views about this?" Allow discussion, but make sure that you finish this section within the time allotted. In the discussion there are two traps into which you must not fall. These correspond to two things which people commonly but incorrectly believe are a necessary part of Christian belief:

- **Evolution**: It is not wise to query the theory of evolution; there is far too much evidence to support it. It cannot be denied that species do evolve over time in a way that enables them to adapt to their environment. What is much more controversial, even among scientists, is the theory that all species have evolved from other species by chance alone – that is, without divine intervention of some kind.

11

- **Creation**: It is not wise to suggest that the first chapter of Genesis is intended to be read as a historical account. In particular, we should not claim that all species were created in a single week. There is overwhelming evidence that species appeared on earth over billions of years – for example when the dinosaurs were here human beings were not. Most Christians regard Genesis chapter 1 as something akin to a poem or a painting; true, but not scientifically true.

Sharing thoughts about creation   (15 mins)

Your discussion should have helped people to see that they do not have to choose between Christian belief and the theory of evolution. Some may still not be confident that God exists, but ask the group to leave that for the moment, and move on to look together at the world.

Ask the group members to each share what is the most awe-inspiring thing they have ever seen (this could be anything from a beautiful rose to the Grand Canyon). Begin with your own answer and then invite each person in turn to share.

When each person has contributed, ask the group as a whole: "If we may presume for a moment that God really does exist, and that the creation really does have a designer, what do you think we might learn about God just by looking at creation?" If they are slow to get going, ask supplementary questions such as "How big is God?", "How powerful is he?", "How clever is he?"

Say to the group that one thing you find awesome about God is the sheer size of his mind. God is able to take in billions of years of history, all the mysteries of the universe, all the fish in the sea, all the detail of everyone's DNA, and so on and so on.

Ask the group how many hairs they think you have on your head. Let them guess then say that Jesus said that God even knows this – for every single person. So where does he store all this information? God seems to be like a giant SATNAV system which knows where every street and every car is and can communicate with all of them at the same time...

People – the summit of creation   (25 mins)

Say to the group that you think that God must be interested in every detail of his creation and that he must derive great pleasure from all of it. But the Bible tells us that there is one part of his creation that delights and concerns him more than any other. Ask the group what they think this is. The answer is us. For God the central focus is on human beings. According to the Bible the creation of the universe, of the earth, and of all living creatures culminated in the creation of man and woman. And according to the Bible God knows us and loves us. He has a unique purpose for each of our lives.

If others have brought a baby picture of themselves collect them together now, and spread them on the floor. Play the game of guessing which picture belongs to each person. If you have only your own picture then put this on the floor and ask people who they think it is. Say that according to the Bible these babies are the apple of God's eye.

Turn to **Genesis 1.26-27**. Ask the group "Why according to these verses are human beings so special?" The answer is because they are made in the image of God. Ask them what they think that might mean, then turn together to **Psalm 8** and ask someone to read verses **3-6.** Ask the group "According to these verses, what is the place that human beings have in creation?"

Now turn to **Psalm 139** and ask someone to read verses **13-14**. Point out to the group what happened when each of them was conceived – inside their mother's body millions of sperm were racing towards a single egg. One particular sperm got there first; had it been any other, they would be an entirely different person. Ask the group, "According to the psalm, who oversaw this process?", or, in other words, "Who designed you to be you?"

Group exercise: Who are you?

Give each person a piece of paper and a pen and ask them to write a list of about 10 characteristics about themselves (these can be quite obvious things, eg *tall, dark haired, good at maths, musical, forgetful* etc.)

After a minute or so collect all the lists in and read them out in turn. Can the group identify the person in question?

Draw out the point of the exercise – each one of us is different but, according to the Bible, each has been designed by God to be who he or she is; we each have our own unique attributes and personalities. Say to the group that you would like to know what they think, especially if they have a handicapped child in their own family. Should we, do they think, abort babies because we know they will be handicapped?

Now summarise by saying something like this:

"You are different from me, you are tall and I am short, you are good with your mind and I am good with my hands, you can paint and I can sing. My DNA is different from your DNA. I am a unique person, and you are a unique person. The question is: why is this?"

Divide the group into pairs. Say that according to the Bible each of us has a unique purpose. Ask the pairs to share with each other what glimpses they have had so far of what that unique purpose is meant to be. For example, you might say, "If you know that you are meant to be a nurse, tell your partner that. If you know that you are a skilled musician, share that."

Allow a brief time for sharing before you interrupt. Then summarise by saying that according to the Bible each one of us has a unique calling or purpose for our lives, and it is up to us to discover what this purpose is. Some people find that this search for meaning can take a lifetime. One thing the Bible does say is that the purpose of each one of us, the thing we have been designed for, is to give pleasure to God. One person gives pleasure to God by the patient way that they cope with great difficulties. Another person gives him pleasure by the courageous way they set about achieving great things. This attitude to life, living in a way which pleases God, is fundamental to what it means to be a Christian.

God loves us – introducing the key verse   (15 mins)

However you manage the time, do not leave this section out! Say to the group that in each week of the course you will be giving them one key verse from the Bible which you hope they will spend a lot of time thinking about.

This week's verse is **Psalm 23.6**. You will have already written it out on a large piece of paper; look at it together now. This verse, like all the key verses, is taken from the NRSV translation:

'Surely goodness and mercy shall follow me all the days of my life, and I shall dwell in the house of the LORD my whole life long.'

Help the group to think about the verse by saying something like:

"All of us have been children, and many of us have children and so know what it means to create people. We also know that it is natural and normal for parents to love their children. It is just as normal and natural for God to love us – each and every one of us. This verse was written by someone who was convinced that God loved him."

This is another of the most fundamental convictions of the Christian life. Christians believe that God exists, that he made us, and that the purpose of our lives is to please him. But perhaps most important of all, every Christian believes 'God loves me.' This is a possibility that group members may never have thought of before. This is what **Psalm 23.6** teaches.

There is a long tradition in the Church of memorising and meditating on verses from the Bible, and many, many people have been helped by doing it. Suggest to the group that it would be good to learn Psalm 23.6 by heart, and ask if they are all happy to do this. If they agree (they probably will) then go ahead with the memorisation. If not, skip the memorising and give them each a card on which to write out the verse.

The easiest way of memorising a verse is to say it out loud, just as children once used to learn their tables. Repeat the verse together as a group. Do this ten times, each time saying the reference before you say the verse, and repeating the reference again at the end. On the tenth time, cover the verse and let the group do it from memory. Try to make this fun and a source of laughter.

Now give people the small cards. Ask them to write the verse on the card and put it in their wallet or purse so that it is easily available. Tell the group that you would like them to set aside time during the week to meditate on this verse. To meditate simply means to think deeply. They will find that the more time they spend pondering the verse the more they will get out of it. Memorisation without meditation is a chore; memorisation with meditation is a joy.

Suggest that you all sit in silence for five minutes, and use the time to think about the verse that you have learned. Is it true? Could it be true that God loves me? Could it be true that his goodness follows me every day? If we believed that this is true, what difference would that make in our lives?

If you are confident that each person in the group has a faith in God, ask them to write out a one sentence prayer based on their meditation. Invite them to read out their prayers in turn. But skip this prayer exercise if you think it would be embarrassing for some.

Homework (5 mins)

Finally, invite the group to turn again to page 7 in the coursebook. Explain that after each session there will be some homework in the form of 4 exercises. The exercises are there to help make practical the things that you have looked at together in the sessions. Give people a few minutes to browse through the coursebook and look at these exercises.

Then explain that the exercises can be used in one of three ways, and ask which they would prefer:

- As suggested in the coursebook you could each choose one exercise and try to complete it before the next session. Those who would like to can do more than one exercise.

- You could choose one exercise together now and decide that everyone will attempt the same one. Some might like to arrange to do the exercise together. Those who are keen could do the others as well.

- You could take more time for the course and decide to use the next meeting to do the exercises as a group. This would double the length of the course, but perhaps people would not mind that.

Beyond Ourselves

Session 2: What's wrong with the world?

This topic is huge, and this session is very important. Allow the group to take its time even if this means finishing off the session at the next meeting. Little will be lost if you get behind and find that you have to omit some of sessions 9 and 10.

Things you will need for this session:

- A whiteboard or flipchart and pens
- Pictures showing sin and suffering (eg from magazines, or from an internet search). Make sure you have more pictures than the number of people in your group. Choose pictures which depict the way people sin against others (eg starvation, violence, bullying, exploitation, homelessness, greed, dishonesty). Choose others which show the way people sin directly against God (contempt, mockery, blasphemy, environmental destruction). And choose some which show suffering caused by natural disasters (earthquakes, volcanic eruptions, flooding).
- Cards for group members to write the key verse on
- A large sheet of paper with Romans 6.23 written out on it.

Introduction   (10 mins)

Begin with a prayer, or simply with a time of silence which will help people still their hearts and minds after a busy day. Be sensitive to where people are in their relationship with God.

Review last week's session (briefly) and then ask the group how they got on with the exercises. If all or most have tackled the exercises and enjoyed them, all is well. If not, then because the exercises are of such importance you will have to say something.

Be gentle with them. Explain the problem as follows, and let them decide what to do about it.

- First talk about the exercises that you yourself have done and why you have found them helpful.

- Then say that because of the way that the course is designed you will all miss out if you just attend the sessions and leave out the exercises.

- Then ask them how they would like to proceed. One possibility is to spend this session doing the exercises from last time together and then move on to session 2 next week. The other possibility is to forget about the session 1 exercises and agree to tackle the exercises starting from session 2. If the group prefer the second option look now at the exercises for session 2 and each decide which exercise you will go for.

Ask for a volunteer to recite last week's key verse (**Psalm 23.6**) and then ask how others have got on with it. Who knows it by heart? Who has been thinking about it? How has the verse helped them?

You may find that many of the group have been thinking about the key verse a great deal and have plenty to share. But, as with the exercises, if the group has overlooked the key verse you will need to say something:

- It is important that you as leader have memorised the verse and that you have something to share about how it has spoken to you.

- The group could decide that after all it does not want to carry on with memorising the key verses – if this is their view, it's best to accept it.

- The group could decide that it does want to carry on memorising, in which case spend a few minutes now helping them go over Psalm 23.6 again.

What has gone wrong? (20 mins)

Introduce today's topic. Explain that
last week you looked at how the world
was created. This week you will be
thinking about what is wrong with the
world.

Spread out your pictures of sin and
suffering for everyone to see. Ask
people to identify which of the
pictures arouses the strongest emotions in them.

Ask if any of them have experienced suffering and allow them to share.
Ask if they have any idea why this has happened to them. Was it their
fault? Was it someone else's fault? Was it bad luck? What do they
think?

Let this lead into a discussion. Probably someone in the group will ask
tough questions – but it is more important that you listen with
compassion than that you give the 'right' answers to the questions. So
try to listen rather than speak (and keep an eye on the time too!).

They will probably raise it, but if they don't, suggest that the key
question is "Why did God create a world with all these problems?" Ask
them what they think.

Explain now that you want to make a distinction between two kinds of
suffering.

- Some suffering has no apparent human cause. It seems to arise from
  the way the universe is. Ask for examples of suffering of this kind.
  Obvious answers are earthquakes, floods, volcanic eruptions, famine,
  sickness, and death.

- Some suffering has an immediate human cause. We suffer because of
  the behaviour of others. Ask for examples of suffering of this kind.
  Obvious answers relate to suffering caused by the violence, lust,
  selfishness of others. Less obvious but equally important answers

relate to suffering caused by the actions and policies of organisations and governments, or from collective mistreatment of the environment – examples might range as widely as pollution, corruption, oppression, global warming...

Then say that this gives rise to two questions. Write these two questions on your board/flipchart.

- Why is the universe as it is?
- Why are people as they are?

Say that these are two very big questions which you will begin to tackle today. Then say that these two questions have always puzzled us, and that the answers to the questions are elusive – perhaps no one really knows. Explain that Jesus was asked similar questions on two occasions. Divide the group into threes and ask them to look at the stories in **Luke 13.1-5** and **John 9.1-7**, and to discuss the answers which Jesus gave.

Bring the group together again and refer them back to the two questions on the board: why is the world as it is, and why are people as they are. Say that there are two possibilities:

- Atheists are right in the answers they give to the big questions. The universe and the people in it are a product of blind, impersonal forces. Nature is red in tooth and claw – that is how it is and we just have to accept it and fight against its worst features. When things get too bad it may make sense to commit suicide.

- Jesus is right. Suffering is pregnant with meaning and understood correctly points the way to salvation and the knowledge of God. The story of Jesus himself demonstrates this – Jesus suffered horribly but following his resurrection his spirit still lives on today. Seen like this our own suffering is always an opportunity for self-discovery and for discovery of God. When others suffer we will alleviate it where we can, but we will always try to bring a message of hope.

Say that you understand why some people choose to be atheists, but that for you this choice feels too pessimistic and you have preferred to explore the Jesus option. As you have tried to understand what Jesus and the Bible say about suffering you have found that this has had a ring of truth. But say also that it is a difficult area, and you do not have all the answers to all the questions.

Then explain that in what remains of today's session you will look first at what Jesus said about the second question, why people are as they are, and then finally you will look at the much misunderstood book of Genesis which directly addresses the two questions which we have written on the board. Say that as you go on you will be very happy to be interrupted by their comments and questions; ask if they have any comments to make now, particularly on what you said about either the atheists being right or Jesus being right.

The flaw in the hearts of men and women   (15 mins)

Start by looking at something Jesus said. Turn to **Mark 7.21-22** and read it together. This is what Jesus says about us: "For it is from within, from the human heart, that evil intentions come: fornication, theft, murder, adultery, avarice, wickedness, deceit, licentiousness, envy, slander, pride, folly."

Write this list of sins on your board, starting with fornication and ending with folly (you may need to explain that fornication means sexual immorality – it comes from the same root as our word pornography – and licentiousness means lawlessness. *The Message* has a good contemporary version of this list).

Look at the list and ask "Has anyone here been a victim, directly or indirectly, of the evil intentions, sexual immorality, greed (etc) of others?" Allow them to share; be ready with examples of your own.

Ask the group if they think that human beings have any choice about being like this. In other words, do people choose to harm one another, or are we programmed to do evil things so that there is no such thing as free will?

Allow them to answer and then say that the Bible's view and in particular the teaching of Jesus is that people do have a choice. We can do good if we want to do good. So if we do bad we are to blame. But add that the Bible also says that we are born with a flaw in our nature. This means that some wrongdoing on our part is inevitable.

Give examples of wrongdoing on your own part which seem to you to be a choice that you made, and wrongdoing which seems to you to have arisen from the way you are. For example, using the list on your board, theft would seem to be a choice, but pride to be something that springs up from the heart. Ask the group whether they agree.

God's laws

Point out that there is a clear connection between the list on the board and the laws (or commandments) of God, which expressly forbid theft, murder, adultery and so on. These commandments were first given by God to Moses in Old Testament times, and they were confirmed by Jesus. But we know that these things are wrong not just because the Bible says they are wrong, but because even our own consciences tell us so. Again ask if they agree.

Explain that the Bible has a simple word which it uses to describe what happens when a person breaks (or ignores!) God's laws; does anyone know what it is? The answer is sin.

Turn to **Romans 3.23** and read it aloud: 'All have sinned and fall short of the glory of God...' Ask the group "According to this verse, which of us have sinned? Which of us have done some of the things that we have written on the board?" The answer is that we all have, even the best of us.

To check this, ask the group if any of them would claim that they have never done any of these things. Do they know of anyone at all who has never done anything wrong? It would seem then that every single one of us is partly responsible for the suffering that spoils our world.

The effect of sin on human relationships   (10 mins)

Say that because sin causes others to suffer, it often
spoils human relationships. Ask people to discuss in
pairs in what ways they observe the results of sin in
the relationships of people close to them, either at
home or at work.

Bring them back together and ask how they think
relationships that have gone wrong can be restored.
Let them respond, but look particularly for the
answer that a relationship which has gone wrong is fully repaired only
when one person sincerely asks for forgiveness and the other is willing
to forgive. Point out that both are necessary.

The effect of sin on our relationship with God   (7 mins)

Explain that according to the Bible our relationship with God works in a
similar way to our relationships with other people.

Turn together to **Isaiah 59.1-2** and ask someone to read it: 'See, the
Lord's hand is not too short to save, nor his ear too dull to hear.
Rather, your iniquities [wrongdoings] have been barriers between you
and your God, and your sins have hidden his face from you so that he
does not hear.'

Explain that in human relationships sin always has the effect of
separating people. The Bible says that it is exactly the same with our
relationship with God. Our sins form a barrier between us and God; the
barrier remains until we say sorry and find his forgiveness.

Ask the group how they think God's forgiveness can be found? Explain
that you will be thinking about this at much greater length in a later
session, but that this week's key verse gives a clue.

24

Introducing the key verse – Romans 6.23 (7 mins)

Introduce this week's key verse, **Romans 6.23**.

'For the wages of sin is death, but the free gift of God is eternal life in Christ Jesus our Lord.'

This verse together with its reference should be displayed for all to see. If the group has accepted the idea of memorising, read it aloud together beginning with the words "Romans 6.23" and continuing by reading the verse. Do this ten times, but on the last time ask the group to say the verse from memory.

Give people the small cards and allow time for them to write the verse out.

Finally turn to **Romans 2.6-10** and ask someone to read it out. The Bible is teaching us that we do have a choice between right and wrong, and that if we choose to do wrong there will be catastrophic consequences for us on the day of judgment. The Bible says much less about hell than most people think, but this is what is meant by hell.

Summarise at this point: To sin is to break the law of God given in the Bible and through conscience. Every human being sins, sometimes through choice, sometimes because of the way we are. Sin separates people from each other and it also separates us from God. Sin has serious consequences in this life and it will have serious consequences on the judgment day which follows death. But it is possible to find forgiveness from God and so avoid that judgment.

Give the group a chance to come back with their questions or comments. Then move on to look at the Genesis story.

Looking at Genesis (13 mins)

Remind the group that the subject of this session is 'What's wrong with the world?'. To answer this, you have been addressing two further questions: 'Why is the universe as it is?' and 'Why are people as they are?'

To help explore these questions, you will look together at one of the most helpful but misunderstood books of the Bible, and see what it has to say about how all this suffering came into being: the book of Genesis.

Ask the group to each say what their favourite poem, painting or piece of sculpture is. When everyone has shared, say that all these art forms communicate truth, but they do not communicate it scientifically. We respond to them with our emotions and identify with them through our experience of life.

Explain that this is probably the best way to read the early chapters of the Bible. They tell stories about the creation of the world, about Adam and Eve, about Noah and the flood, and the tower of Babel. In these stories we see the world as it is, we see ourselves, and we see each other. In that sense they are full of truth.

Explain that although virtually all Christians believe that the story of Jesus in the New Testament is historical, only some Christians believe this about Genesis. Indeed to view Genesis as history is a fairly recent stance. Most Christians see Genesis in a different way, full of truth but more akin to poetry than to history.

Say to the group that you propose to take them through the chapters step by step, summarising the key points. If they have Bibles they may like to follow the story, but you will do most of the talking. Questions can come later.

These notes summarise the talk that you will now give:

- **Genesis 1.27** – God created man and woman
- **Genesis 1.31** – God saw that his creation was very good, including man and woman.
- **Genesis 2.16** – The moral dimension is introduced: God gives Adam and Eve a commandment or law.
- **Genesis 3.1-6** – The serpent tempts the man and the woman and they break the commandment.

Explain that throughout the Bible temptation is personalised. Look briefly at **Luke 22.3-6**, where the tempter is called Satan, and at **1 John 5.19**, where Satan is said to have great influence in our world.

Sin has its origin in temptation. The Bible does not lay responsibility for temptation at our door, but says that the inner voice of temptation has a satanic origin. Ask if anyone in the group has ever experienced overwhelming temptation. As leader, be prepared to share your own experience if no one else does.

Continuing in Genesis:

- **Genesis 3.7** – One effect of sin is that it produces shame and guilt in those who have sinned. Ask if anyone in the group has ever felt ashamed.
- **Genesis 3.8** – Another effect of sin is that something goes wrong in the relationship between man and God.

Next we are offered another reason why people suffer. We know that good parents discipline their children and that sometimes this is unpleasant. Genesis says that God is the same – because we sin, we are disciplined. Two aspects of that suffering are mentioned.

- **Genesis 3.16** – One aspect of God's discipline is that we experience difficulty in child-bearing; the continuation of human life is not easy.
- **Genesis 3.17-19** - Another aspect of God's discipline is that our work is often hard and back-breaking; the maintenance of life on earth is also not easy.

Say that it is important not to misunderstand this. If I have a hard time in my work or family life, this is not a direct punishment for something I have personally done. This discipline from God is a discipline on the human race as a whole. The whole human race suffers because the human race as a whole has sinned. Because I too have sinned, I cannot complain that this is unjust.

Finally Genesis teaches, as the memory verse says, that it is as a direct consequence of human sin and our separation from God, who is both the origin and source of life, that we die:

- **Genesis 3.22-24** - The final effect of sin is that we will no longer be able to eat from the tree of life. One day every man and every woman must die. Because mankind sins, mankind dies.

Why people suffer   (8 mins)

Say that you have looked carefully at Genesis because it gives so much insight as to why our world is so full of suffering, and that you would now like to draw some conclusions.

There are four reasons given in the Bible to explain why people suffer. Three of these can be found in Genesis:

- People suffer because of God's discipline; the discipline of suffering is built into the world. Suffering draws our attention to the separation we experience when we are alienated from God, and to the need to put things right in our relationship with God.

- People suffer both directly and indirectly because of the sins of others. This accounts for the vast majority of human suffering.

- People suffer because of the activity of Satan. Satan can and sometimes does cause acute suffering. We don't know how or why.

The Bible teaches in many places that:

- Suffering sometimes serves as a kind of test. Indeed the whole of life is a test: all kinds of things happen to us, and the question is how will we respond? We can all think of people who have suffered hugely but have borne it so well that they shine through the suffering. People like this will often tell you that God has been very close to them in the suffering – many say that suffering has brought benefits that could not have come any other way.

Finally

- As with the case of the man born blind in **John 9**, God sometimes steps in to relieve or remove suffering. This sudden defeat of suffering brings glory to God, and points forward to the time when God promises to end all human suffering. The resurrection of Jesus shows that even death is to be ultimately defeated.

Groups will vary greatly in their response to this discussion. Some will listen carefully and largely accept what you say, but others will dispute everything. If your group is inclined to disagree, make sure you give them space and listen to them respectfully. If you run out of time, express the hope that they will save up their questions and ask them in subsequent sessions.

Beyond Ourselves

Session 3: Who is Jesus?

No one can become a Christian or receive the Holy Spirit unless they are first convinced that Jesus is who he claimed to be, and no one will reach this conviction unless they first hear the New Testament story. So in this session the group is going to spend a lot of time looking at the gospels. As you prepare for this session, pray for the group members that as they do this God will open their eyes and help them to see who Jesus really is.

Things you will need for this session :

- A flipchart or board & pens
- Medium sized post-it notes, with scripture references written on them
- John 1.12 written out on a large sheet of paper
- Bibles
- Small cards on which group members can write out the key verse.

Introduction   (10 mins)

Ask one of the group members to open with a prayer, or simply invite the group to still their hearts and minds in a time of silence, as appropriate. Then briefly summarise the main points of sessions 1 and 2. And if you are memorising the key verses, ask for two volunteers to recite the first two.

Then give people a chance to say how they have experienced this week's exercises.

Finally introduce today's topic by explaining that this session is about Jesus – beliefs about Jesus are fundamental to the Christian faith.

Who is Jesus? (20 mins)

On your board/flipchart write out in large letters the words WHO IS JESUS? Then ask each member of the group to say how they think they would have answered this question when they were eight years old.

Let each person answer and then say that the aim of this session is to give us evidence by which we can form an adult view of the question "Who is Jesus?"

If needed, give a very brief overview of Jesus's life, perhaps saying something like this:

"Jesus lived a little over 2,000 years ago. The Bible tells how he was born in Bethlehem and was raised by his mother Mary and her husband Joseph, a carpenter. He worked as a carpenter himself in a small town called Nazareth until he was about 30. He was then baptised by John the Baptist, after which he started to teach with great authority and to perform many miracles all around Judea. His ministry lasted about 3 years before he was arrested, put on trial and crucified. Three days later he rose from the dead, appearing to his followers for a period of 40 days before ascending to heaven in their sight."

Explain that these are the bare facts but that the Bible provides us with much more detail: there are four accounts of the life of Jesus in the Bible, known as the four gospels. They contain not only the words and actions of Jesus, but also the reactions and opinions of many who encountered him.

Tell the group that you will now look at some passages from two of the gospels to get an idea of how some of the people who actually met him answered the question 'Who is Jesus?'

Have the following scripture references written on separate post-it notes:

Matthew 7.28-29
Matthew 8.28-34
Matthew 9.18-34

Matthew 14.22-33	Mark 11.8-10	Luke 20.1-8
Matthew 16.13-17	Luke 2.25-28	John 1.10-12
Matthew 27.45-54	Luke 7.11-16	John 5.39-40
Mark 3.11-1	Luke 7.17-26	John 6.60-68
Mark 6.1-6	Luke 7.36-50	

Ask everyone to turn in their Bibles to the first scripture, **Matthew 7.28-29**.

Ask: "These verses show some people coming to conclusions about Jesus. What conclusion did they reach? "

The answer is that 'Jesus taught with great authority.' Write this on the post-it note and stick it onto your board.

Now that they have done an example together, put them into groups of two or three, and divide up the references among them (if your group is small you may wish to leave out some of the passages). Ask them to read the passages they have been given, look for the conclusions that different people reached about Jesus, write them on the post-it note and stick it on the board. Warn them that in some passages some people come to one conclusion and some to another.

Then say "So we see that people had all kinds of opinions about Jesus, just as we did when we were eight years old. These opinions mattered. Those who believed that Jesus was the Son of God ended up by giving their lives to him. Those who rejected his claims remained relatively untouched by him. It will be the same for us, which is why it is so important that we think carefully about the question 'Who is Jesus?'"

Ask the group how they would define a Christian. Let them answer but help them to see that any definition of a Christian which leaves Jesus out is an inadequate definition. Examples might be:

- A Christian is someone who has been baptised
- A Christian is someone who goes to church
- A Christian is someone who believes in God
- A Christian is someone who tries to live by the teachings of the Bible

Christians do all the things listed above, but the essence of what it means to be a Christian is to live a life which is centred on Jesus. So offer some better definitions:

- A Christian is someone who believes in Jesus
- A Christian is someone who has put their trust in Jesus
- A Christian is someone who has a personal relationship with Jesus
- A Christian is someone who has decided to follow Jesus and be his disciple

Explain that if someone is to make a decision to become a Christian, this means they must first decide what they think about Jesus.

Reasons to believe in Jesus – his miracles   (15 mins)

Suggest to the group that if they have time they should try to read John's gospel at a single sitting. If they do this, they will see that throughout the gospel the question 'Who is Jesus?' is the main issue. They will see that John, and other writers of the New Testament who had lived with Jesus, were convinced that Jesus was none other than God himself in human form.

Ask the group why they think that the writers of the New Testament believed this? Why did they believe that Jesus was divine, the Son of God, unique amongst all the people who had ever lived? Why did they personally choose to follow and even to worship him?

Let them answer, and then say that you will spend the rest of this session exploring this question.

The first and most obvious answer is that people followed Jesus because of his miracles. No one else in history has ever performed miracles on this scale or anywhere near it.

Turn with the group to **John 2.1-11**, which tells the story of Jesus's first public miracle. Focus on verse 11 and observe that his disciples believed in him because of the miracle. Two of those early disciples were John, the writer of the gospel, and Peter, the best known of Jesus' disciples.

Then put the group into pairs and ask each pair to read **Matthew chapter 8**, which describes just one day in the life of Jesus. As they read the chapter they should ask themselves 'If we had been with Jesus on that day what would we have believed about him at the end of it?'

People may ask questions about the reliability of the Bible account. If so, say that this is a good question and that it will be covered in the next session.

Reasons to believe in Jesus – his claims   (11 mins)

The second reason why the disciples and the writers of the Bible believed in Jesus was because of his claims. It wasn't what others said about Jesus that was remarkable. It is what he said, and obviously believed, about himself.

First turn with the group to **Matthew 16.13-17.** Jesus asked Peter what he thought about him, and Peter said "You are the Son of God." Peter believed this because he had been with Jesus and seen what Jesus could do; but notice too that Jesus did not deny what Peter said. Ask the group what this passage tells us about Jesus' view of himself.

Then turn with the group to **John 20.28-30** where Thomas, like Peter, identified Jesus as being God. Jesus said that a great blessing would come to all who reached the same conclusion. Ask the group again "What does this passage say about Jesus' attitude to himself?"

Finally turn to **John 14.1-6**. The disciples are troubled and do not know what to believe. Jesus says "Believe in me, because I am the way to God. Indeed I and my Father are one." Ask the group what this passage tells us about Jesus' view of himself? Then ask what we would think if someone made those claims for himself today? Finally ask the group to turn to the quotation from C S Lewis on page 20 in their coursebooks and ask someone to read this out. Do they think that Lewis is right?

Reasons to believe in Jesus – his teaching   (12 mins)

Explain that another reason why so many accept Jesus' claims is because of the profundity of what he taught. If Jesus was a fraud it really seems incredible that he should be the author of such new and deep moral teaching.

Turn together to **Luke 6.2-49** and give each person time to read it (if not everyone has a Bible, put them into pairs). Point out that this passage consists entirely of sayings from Jesus, and suggest that they try to let the words speak to them as they read.

Give them about 6 minutes and then ask "Was there anything in that teaching that struck you and seemed relevant to your life?"

Point out that there have many other great teachers who have spoken with great insight about the human condition – people like Confucius or the Buddha, Gandhi or Nelson Mandela – but that what these teachers all shared, and Jesus apparently lacked, is a modest view of their own importance.

Reasons to believe in Jesus – his sinless life   (5 mins)

Ask the group to think of someone they know well and admire deeply. Ask them how they would describe this person. Then ask them to compare this with what John and Peter said about Jesus.

Turn first to **John 1.14** and ask the group what it was that John said about Jesus? The answer is that he was full of grace and truth.

Then look at **1 Peter 2.21-23** and ask the group what it was that Peter said about Jesus? The answer is that he led a sinless life.

Ask the group "If you had lived with Jesus, as Peter and John had, what conclusions do you think you would have reached about him?"

Reasons to believe in Jesus – his resurrection   (2 mins)

Finally say that above all the reason why Peter and John and the others believed in Jesus was because they saw him alive after they knew he had died. This is so extraordinary and so important that it will be the main subject in the next session. Can we believe this really happened? If it did then it will be very easy to believe in Jesus.

Key verse for this week   (10 mins)

Finally ask the group to look at **John chapter 1**. Begin with verse 18. Remind the group of the discussions you had about the existence or non-existence of God and about the mystery of suffering. Say that sometimes the subject of God can seem too big for us, and the questions too hard to understand, never mind answer. Is there a God? If so who made him? Why does God allow suffering? These are very difficult questions and it is not surprising that some wish to remain agnostic when confronted by them.

But verse 18 suggests that there is a simple way to cut through the questions and get to the answer: all we have to do is look at Jesus and make up our minds about him. If Jesus is who he claims to be, then the bigger questions become much easier to resolve. All we need do is look at what Jesus said about them.

Next look at verses 10 and 11. Jesus came into the world. There was plenty of evidence that what Jesus had to say was true, and we have looked at some of it. But still many people rejected him. This remains true today. There are lots of reasons to believe in Jesus, but many people still do not do so.

Then look at verse 12. John, the writer of this gospel, is one of those who did believe. He knew Jesus, he lived and talked with him, and he believed in him. And because he believed, John became a child of God. For John, God stopped being a remote figure and became a personal father.

Learn **John 1.12** together, or write it out on cards, or both as the group has decided:

'But to all who received him, who believed in his name, he gave power to become children of God.'

Encourage them to continue with the exercises in the coursebooks and to meditate on the key verses.

Be aware that if you are to lead this group well you will need to get some one on one time with the group members. Now might be a good opportunity to fix some appointments.

Beyond Ourselves

Session 4: Is there life after death?

> **Things you will need for this session :**
>
> - A flipchart or board & pens
> - John 3.16 written out on a large sheet of paper
> - Bibles
> - Small cards on which group members can write out the key verse.

Life after death   (15 mins)

Ask one of the group members to open with a prayer, or invite the group to still their hearts and minds in a time of silence, as appropriate. Then ask which of the exercises they have tried, and give them an opportunity to share how they got on.

Now ask the group what they think will happen to them when they die. Let them answer, and then say something like this: "My belief is that after I die God will not forget me but will remake me with a new body, and that I will then be in his presence forever. This belief is fundamental to what it means to be a Christian." Explain that you believe this because you believe that Jesus has already experienced resurrection, and because Jesus said that what happened to him will also happen to us.

Explain that in this session you will be assessing the evidence for the resurrection of Jesus and for our own future resurrection.

Someone may say that they do not want to live on after death because the idea of living forever does not appeal to them. Reassure them that life after death (which Jesus called eternal life) is not simply a continuation of life on earth with its frequent pain and periods of boredom. Eternal life is the life that God lives, not the life which we live. Just as a baby cannot understand life outside the womb until he or she leaves the womb, so we cannot understand eternal life until we experience it. It will be life in a totally different dimension to the one we know now, and will bring a fulfilment we have never known.

Then say that, before you get on to the reasons why Christians believe that there is life after death, you want to return briefly to the subject of suffering. This is because there is a link between the subject of suffering and the subject of life after death. Remind the group that all people suffer, but that some suffer far more than others.

Ask who in the group feels that they have suffered very little, and who feels that they have suffered a lot. Choose two people, one from each end of the spectrum. Ask these two to say which of them they feel has been the most fortunate. And ask the others which of these two people they would rather be.

Your reason for asking this is partly to allow more time for a discussion of the big subject of suffering, but you are also wanting to make a point. It is obvious that life is not at all fair. Bad things do happen to good people. If there is no life after death, then those who suffer most in this life are most to be pitied. But if there is life after death, then suffering in this life is not necessarily as bad as it seems. It may even be the best way to prepare for the next life.

Say to the group that Jesus is the one who suffered most. He was crucified at the age of 30 in horrible circumstances, but he did not complain, because his suffering had a purpose. This purpose was revealed by his resurrection.

The story of the resurrection of Jesus   (15 mins)

Explain that among all the things that Jesus said and did, the thing that makes him unique is the fact that he died and then reappeared alive. Ask the group if they personally believe that the resurrection of Jesus was a historical event? If they say that they do, ask them what difference this makes to them. If they say that they don't believe this, ask them what difference they think it would make if they did?

Say that the main evidence for the resurrection of Jesus comes from the writers of the New Testament, all of whom say that after his death Jesus appeared to his disciples, spoke with them and did things with them.

Turn to **Acts 1.3**, which says that there were many resurrection appearances, and that they extended over a period of 40 days. Tell the group that you would like to take a close look at the very first of these appearances as it is described in Luke's gospel.

Turn to **Luke 24**. Begin by explaining the background to this chapter. Jesus had died in a horrific way on the cross, and his body had been placed in a tomb. The disciples, especially the men, were bewildered and frightened. How could the wonderful life of Jesus end in such a way? Perhaps now the same thing would happen to them?

Make sure each person has sight of a Bible, and work through this passage together. Then read out the following sections from **Luke 24** and ask the group the questions. Move on quite quickly. Your aim at this point is not to have a discussion but simply to help the group to understand what the passage is saying:

- Verses 1-7. Who were the first people to become aware of the resurrection of Jesus?

- Verses 8-11. How did the male disciples respond to what the women told them? Is this what you would have expected?

- Verse 36. How did Jesus convince the men that he was still alive?

- Verses 37-40. How were the disciples persuaded that they were not seeing a ghost?

- Verse 41. How did the disciples react once they had been able to touch Jesus?

- Verses 41-42. How did Jesus further demonstrate that he was actually alive? If you had been in that room would you have been convinced?

At this point say to the group that you have looked at just one story about the resurrection of Jesus – but that the New Testament has many such stories. Jesus did not just appear to the disciples once, he appeared many times. If these stories are true, this has profound implications. If death was not the end for Jesus, then perhaps death will not be the end for us either. So the question is – is there enough evidence to make us believe that the four Gospel writers are telling us the truth when they claim that Jesus was seen alive after he was undoubtedly dead?

Before you move on ask the group what they think about this.

Evidence for the truth of the story   (30 mins)

Four accounts

Remind the group that in the Bible we have four accounts of the life, death and resurrection of Jesus. These are written by Matthew, Mark, Luke and John. When we read them we find that they differ slightly and even seem to contradict each other on some of the details. Probably the biggest  clash between the four gospel stories is the one between the story which we have just looked at in Luke 24, and the account of the same incident in Matthew 28. Look together at **Luke 24.1-10** and **Matthew 28.1-10** and try to piece together what actually happened.

Suggest to the group that this difference between the stories is exactly what you would expect. If a major story broke today, four newspapers would report it slightly differently. If the four versions were all exactly the same, we would suspect the story of being made up and then copied from one paper to another. It is when the details differ that we know that the essence of the story is true – that there has indeed been an earthquake or an air crash or whatever. In the same way we know that something really did happen in Jerusalem after Jesus died.

A reliable text

Some people have argued that what Matthew, Mark, Luke and John wrote is not what we read today. They say that the church might have altered the Bible at a later stage because they wanted people to believe that Jesus was much more than he really was. Explain why this is extremely unlikely:

The original versions of the four accounts were not printed but hand written. Copies were then made of the originals, and then copies of copies. This went on for centuries until the age of printing. So in theory someone could have made a copy which was inaccurate, either accidentally or deliberately. And this error could have been passed on to subsequent copies.

The reason we know that this did not happen is that 2500 early copies of the New Testament have been preserved, a sample of the huge number which have been made throughout the centuries. All these copies can be dated accurately. The earliest copy we have of part of the New Testament dates from 110 AD and the earliest complete copy dates from 250 AD.

If these 2500 copies were found to differ markedly from one another this would suggest that the original had been altered often and by many people. But in fact the 2500 copies are almost identical. The only possible explanation for this is that the 2500 copies are all more or less the same as the original. The version of the gospels that we have is reliable.

Now explain that the same argument is routinely applied by classical scholars to other works written at the same time as the New Testament – for example the accounts of Caesar's wars or the speeches of Cicero. Scholars carefully compare the surviving manuscripts and are able to say with confidence that by and large the original has survived the copying process. In fact the manuscript evidence for the New Testament is far more extensive than for any other contemporary work.

Eye witnesses

Some have argued that Matthew, Mark, Luke and John were not eye witnesses, and some have even suggested that they wrote many decades after the events they describe. If this were true it would make them more like historians than journalists, and would mean that they were not in a position to really know what happened.

But this hypothesis is also far-fetched. Turn with the group to **Luke 1.1-4** and ask the group what this tells us about Luke's gospel. Luke was not himself an eye-witness of the resurrection, but he obviously knew people who were.

Then turn to **John 12.23**, which is one of several places in which the writer describes 'the disciple whom Jesus loved. 'Look too at **John 21.20-25**, which says that this disciple is himself the author of the gospel. The writer of the gospel was there when it happened; and there is every reason to believe that this was the disciple John. Explain that some think that the gospel could have been written not by John himself but by someone who knew him extremely well; this is a possibility.

We know that Mark's gospel predates Luke because Luke obviously got some of his material from Mark. Was Mark an eye-witness? It is impossible to tell, but from the prominence his gospel gives to Peter it seems very likely that Mark knew Peter personally. It is only Matthew's gospel which cannot be clearly linked to eye-witness accounts.

Liars?

Say that if we accept that in the New Testament we have carefully preserved eye-witness accounts of the life of Jesus, then this still leaves another possibility. Perhaps the eye-witnesses were not reliable – perhaps they did not tell the truth or perhaps they were mistaken?

Consider together the possibility that the eye-witnesses were liars. Turn to **Acts 4.1-20** and put people in pairs to read it. The passage tells of something that happened a few weeks after the resurrection when Peter and John, the most prominent of the eye-witnesses, told their story in Jerusalem. Ask the pairs to decide if it is conceivable that John and Peter would have behaved like this if they knew that the story of the resurrection was a lie?

Then bring the group together and turn to **Acts 2.32,** which is part of the address which Peter gave to the crowd in Jerusalem about six weeks after the resurrection. We know that Peter was risking his life by declaring publicly that he had seen Jesus alive, and that eventually he would suffer imprisonment, beating, and execution for doing so. Ask the group why he would have said this if he knew it was not true?

Point out that it is also interesting that Peter was saying these things in Jerusalem only a few hundred yards away from the tomb where Jesus' body had been placed. If Jesus was still dead we may reasonably wonder why those who were opposed to Peter did not go to the tomb and produce the body?

Mistaken?

Say now that this leaves one more possibility. Peter and John and the other eye-witnesses were not liars, but perhaps they were mistaken, or perhaps the people who wrote the story down were mistaken about what they had said. The events which the New Testament describes

happened when they were young men, but the writing down happened when they were much older. Could their memories have served them badly, or could they have been misinformed?

Choose the oldest person present, and ask him or her to describe something which happened many years ago. Then ask the rest of the group to discuss whether or not the events described did really take place.

It should be obvious that the essentials of the story have been reported faithfully, but that some of the details may have changed with the passing of time. It must be the same for the New Testament stories. But who would argue that the resurrection is a detail? The resurrection is the essence of the Christian story.

A final piece of evidence   (15 mins)

Point out that so far we have been thinking mainly about the gospel writers, Matthew, Mark, Luke and John. But perhaps the most important piece of evidence comes not from the gospels but from the writing of St Paul.

The evidence from Paul

Turn to **1 Corinthians 15.1-8**, part of Paul's letter to the church in Corinth, and explain that although experts do argue about the authorship and dating of the gospels, everyone agrees that Paul's letter to Corinth was written in 56 AD, about 25 years after the resurrection itself.

A few years before, Paul had gone to Corinth and there he had founded a new church. They were a bunch of ordinary people just like your group, but probably more numerous. Say to the group that you would like them to imagine that it is the year 56, and that you are that group of Christians in Corinth. Paul has been gone for a couple of years now, but you have written to him and his reply to the letter has just arrived.

Why did you write to Paul? Lots of reasons, but one was that some members of the church have died. Paul had said that it would be OK if this happened, because they would go straight to God. But you are having doubts. Suppose this is not true? Suppose when you die you are just dead? So you wrote to Paul about this, hoping for reassurance.

Ask the group to imagine that Paul's letter has just arrived, and say that you are going to read his answer. To get the full answer, we would have to read the whole of chapter 15. But for now ask one person to read verses 1-8 and another to read verses 12-19.

After the reading, ask the group two questions. Firstly, have they understood what Paul is saying; and secondly have they been persuaded by his argument? Let them answer, and if you need to, summarise what he says as follows:

- If your friends are not with God but just dead in their graves, then there is no such thing as life after death and I, Paul, am completely wrong in everything I have been saying. Why do you imagine that I say such things if I do not believe them to be true?

- If there is no life after death then Jesus is still in his tomb in Jerusalem.

- But I know that Jesus is not in his tomb. He was seen alive by many people, many of whom I know personally.

- Jesus proved to me that he is alive by appearing to me also.

- As Jesus is undoubtedly alive and we are quite sure that this is true, then there must be life after death.

In this passage Paul gives the evidence which persuaded him that Jesus really had been raised from death. Paul had not been one of Jesus' disciples and so had nothing to prove. And he had been in an excellent position to check the evidence because he was personally acquainted with all the people whose names he mentions. It is hard to believe that Paul got this wrong, and hard to believe that he made the story up – he, like Peter, was severely persecuted for his faith.

The evidence from personal experience

If you have time, turn to **Ephesians 1.2**, where Jesus is spoken of as someone who can bring grace and peace into people's lives. That Jesus was alive and active long after he had been crucified was the core belief of the early church, which had by now been expanding rapidly all over the known world. It was this belief in the resurrection that gave the church its strength and made it so successful. It is hard to believe that the growth of Christianity was based on an event that never happened and an experience of Jesus that was not real.

You could ask the group to think of other events in history which changed the world, for example the visions of Mohammed, or the healing of Bernadette at Lourdes, or the Battle of Hastings, and ask whether it would be wise to claim that these events never happened? Point out that *something* happened to get Christianity going. If it was not the resurrection then what was it – no one has ever come up with a plausible alternative explanation.

Faith and doubt, and this week's key verse   (10 mins)

Now turn to **John 20.24-29**. Invite someone to read it and then ask: "What do you think of Thomas' initial reluctance to believe in the resurrection? What do you think of verse 29 – does it seem fair to be asked to believe because of what someone else has told you?"

Choose the strongest looking member of the group and ask him to stand a little way behind you (or, if you are heavy, ask the smallest member to take your part). Ask him "If I fall backwards will you promise to catch me?" If he says yes, ask the group how you can test out his answer. They should suggest that this can be done only by believing him, trusting him and demonstrating that trust by falling backwards to see if he does indeed catch you. Ask the group what will happen if you refuse to believe that he will catch you and just remain standing? The answer is that absolutely nothing will happen.

Point out that doubt does not have immediate negative consequences, but neither does it get you anywhere. It is only believing that gets results. Having said that, take a risk and fall backwards. If you aren't caught, the session ends here!

Reinforce to the group that to be a Christian means to put your trust in what you are told about Jesus – which is what Thomas failed to do. There will always be those who demand proof, as Thomas did, but real Christians are those who have decided that there is enough evidence for them to go for it. When they do, they find that Jesus catches them – just as the strong group member caught you.

Help the group to think a bit further about this by explaining that it's a bit like sky-diving – you have to trust the guy who tells you your parachute will open. The parachute is no use at all unless you jump. Ask the group if anyone has ever tried sky diving? What did it feel like when they jumped? And what did it feel like when the parachute opened?

What else do Christians believe about Jesus?   (5 mins)

Explain that there are other important things that Christians believe about Jesus which you do not have time to explore in detail. But reassure them that if we believe the resurrection to be true it is quite easy to believe that these other things are also true.

Some of these core beliefs are as follows, and you may have time to look at some of them:

Acts 1.6-11 – Christians believe that Jesus ascended into heaven.

The resurrection appearances of Jesus eventually came to an end. Of course, each appearance of Jesus ended with another disappearance. In this passage Jesus makes it clear that this will be his last disappearance. They will never again see him on earth until he returns at the end of time.

Matthew 28.18 – Christians believe that Jesus is now Lord of heaven and earth. Jesus said that he had been given all authority in heaven and earth, and Christians believe that he still has this authority. This is very good news, for it means that the person who oversees our lives and our futures is Jesus. Jesus taught his followers to use his authority when they prayed, and this is why Christians today pray in the name of Jesus.

Acts 2.38 – Christians believe that Jesus sends His Holy Spirit to all who believe in him. The Holy Spirit is God, just as Jesus is God. The Holy Spirit is God living with us and in us. Learning how to receive the Holy Spirit, how to be filled by the Spirit, and how to live in step with the Spirit is also a big part of the Christian life.

1 Thessalonians 4.16-17 – Christians believe that Jesus will return to judge the world. The Christian life is lived between two great events, the resurrection of Jesus and the return of Jesus in glory. As we look back to the resurrection so we look forward to his return.

Key verse   (5 mins)

This week's key verse is **John 3.16**:

'For God so loved the world that he gave his only Son, so that everyone who believes in him may not perish but may have eternal life.'

Hand out the blank cards for people to write the key verse on. Learn the verse together in the usual way.

And encourage people to keep on memorising and meditating on the key verses.

Beyond Ourselves

Session 5: The death of Jesus

Things you will need for this session:

- A large piece of paper or card with **1 Peter 3.18** written out on it.
- A film of the life of Jesus so that you can watch the story of the crucifixion
- Bibles
- Small cards on which group members can write out the key verse.
- Pens and paper for the group members
- 2 garments – one old and dirty, one new and smart

Introduction   (5 mins)

Open with a prayer or by keeping a time of silence. Then enquire how people got on with the exercises during the week.

Revision is always helpful – so ask 4 volunteers to recite (or read, if you are not memorising them) the 4 key verses given so far. Encourage everyone to continue to meditate on them.

Looking at the story of the cross   (10 mins)

This can be done in one of two ways. The best way is to obtain a film of the life of Jesus and watch an excerpt together which shows how he died. Alternatively, read the account of the crucifixion from Matthew's gospel (**Matthew 27.27-54**), sharing the reading between several people.

Ask each member of the group to describe their feelings as they watched the film or read the story.

Explain that today you will be looking at the meaning of the death of Jesus. What was going on when Jesus, the Son of God, was being crucified? Obviously there was a painful and terrible death; but was there a deeper meaning? Ask the group to give their opinions – what do they think the cross of Jesus was all about?

Explain that Christians have traditionally understood the cross in three different ways, each of which finds strong support in the Bible. Some people find one explanation more helpful than others; this does not matter, because they are just different ways of helping us to understand the same thing.

1. The cross – an act of forgiveness (15 mins)

The first way to look at the cross is to see it as an act of forgiveness. Read **Luke 23.34** and explain that Jesus is speaking to his Father from the cross about the people who had put him there. Ask the group who these people were – who contributed to the killing of Jesus?

Possible answers include:

- the Jewish religious leaders
- Pilate, the Roman governor
- the crowd, who cried "Crucify him!"
- Judas, who betrayed him
- Peter, who denied him
- the soldiers who crucified him
- all of us, because we all sin

As Jesus hung on the cross he asked his Father to forgive all these people. Ask the group if any of them have had the experience of forgiving someone who has done them a serious wrong, or if anyone has struggled to forgive such a person?

Now ask each person to write two things on a piece of paper (explain that they will not be asked to share what they write):

- What is the worst thing ever done to you by another person?
- What is the worst thing that you yourself ever did?

Continue by thinking about the first of the things we have written, that is the things that have been done to us. Give an example of a bad thing that was done to you and say that the normal, healthy response when someone treats us badly is anger. Say that the thing that has been done to you makes you feel angry, and ask if any of them also feels angry about the way someone has treated them. If anyone does feel angry, support them. Ask the group how they think God feels when he sees how human beings sometimes behave? Look together at **Romans 2.8-9**: God too feels anger.

Now ask, "When you feel angry, how do handle your anger?" Ask if anyone in the group has ever lost their temper with someone who has angered them. Has anyone has ever taken revenge? Does anyone find themselves sulking when they are angry?

Then say that the cross shows us a better way of handling our anger, the way of forgiveness. Turn to page 31 in the coursebooks, where you will find a true story about forgiveness. Divide into pairs to read and discuss this story.

Bring the group together again and ask them to think now about the worst thing they ever did. Tell the group about something wrong which you once did, and ask "Would God be right to be angry with me because of this?" What do they think?

The answer according to the Bible is that of course God is right to be angry, but that the cross is God's way of saying "I choose to handle my anger by forgiving you." In his prayer on the cross Jesus, the Son of God, asked his Father not to hold anything against the people who had put him there, and this includes each one of us. So from the cross God is saying "Whatever it is that you have done, I forgive it."

Point out that it is one thing to be forgiven, but another thing to have accepted that forgiveness. A Christian is someone who has accepted the forgiveness that Jesus offered from the cross. Ask the group what they think would show that someone really had accepted that forgiveness?

Let them answer, and look for the two following main points:

- We demonstrate that we have accepted our forgiveness by the love which we show for Jesus, the one who has suffered so that we might be forgiven.

- We show that we have accepted our forgiveness by our willingness to forgive those who have done wrong to us.

Say that you find it helpful to visualise this. Ask everyone to stand and close their eyes, and imagine that they are watching Jesus being crucified. Help them to visualise the scene:

"It is dark and there are three crosses. Jesus is on the central cross. A rough crown made from thorns has been thrust onto his head. A notice has been nailed to the cross which says 'The king of the Jews'. Large nails have been driven through his ankles and his wrists to fasten him to the cross, and the life is beginning to flow from him. He is getting weaker and weaker, and finding it harder and harder to breathe."

Invite each group member to imagine that Jesus is looking directly at them; encourage them try to make eye contact with him. Tell them,

"Jesus is saying 'Father forgive him/her' – he is forgiving you and accepting you as his brother or sister despite all your failings. Jesus loves you. He is asking his Father not to hold anything against you. He is welcoming you into the Kingdom of God. How will you respond to Jesus?" Do you feel a love for Jesus? How will you express that love?"

Ask them to keep their eyes closed, and now change the picture. Say that in front of them now is not Jesus but the person who has most harmed them. Then tell them,

"You are no longer in that crowd; imagine that now you are on the cross with Jesus. Put your body into his body and feel his pain. Now look out from the

53

cross through the eyes of Jesus. Do you see the person who has hurt you standing there in the crowd? Will you pray, as Jesus prayed, "Father forgive them"? "Father, Jesus died for me to set me free and I am asking you, Father, to set this person free because I know that Jesus has died for them too. Father, I release this person to you'."

Suggest that if they can they should pray this prayer right now. Repeat the prayer out loud yourself and pray it slowly so that they can join in but suggest that they pray silently in their hearts.

2. The cross – satisfying the justice of God   (20 mins)

So, the first way of understanding the cross is to see it as an act of forgiveness. You are now going to move on to a second way of looking at the cross.

Ask the group what happens when someone breaks the law of this country and gets caught? The answer is that the person will receive the due punishment.

It is exactly the same with the law of God. If we break God's laws there is a due punishment.

Ask the group what they think the due punishment for breaking God's laws is? Ask what will happen to us if we are murderers, adulterers, liars, thieves, or lovers of ourselves and not of God? The answer was given in the key verse for session 2 – the due punishment for sin is death. Ask the group how they feel about this.

The natural response is that the punishment is too harsh. Maybe Bin Laden or Hitler deserve to die, but surely not me! But the Bible teaches that God is so perfect, so holy, that any sin at all puts us fundamentally at odds with God, who is himself the source of life. Remind them of the story in Genesis where Adam and Eve lose their life because they disobeyed one simple command from God.

Now put the group into threes or fours and ask each group to look at **1 Peter 3.18**. Ask each group what this verse says about the death of Jesus on the cross.

A practical demonstration

When they report back they should have discovered that on the cross Jesus himself was suffering for our sins. Jesus was taking the penalty for sin in place of each one of us.

Illustrate this by asking for two volunteers – one represents Jesus and the other represents himself or herself.

Suppose this second volunteer is called Jack. Provide Jack with a very old and dirty coat or shirt and ask him to wear it. Say that because Jack has broken God's laws many times then this is how God sees him.

Provide the person who is playing Jesus with an extremely smart new coat or shirt. Because Jesus is God's Son, and because Jesus led a sinless life, this is how God sees Jesus.

Now ask the group "What happened on the cross?". The answer is that Jesus was exchanging garments with Jack. So instruct the person who represents Jesus to ask Jack if he would like to swap garments. Point out that not everybody accepts this invitation – but everyone can if they want to. Jesus should then take off Jack's coat and replace it with his own coat. Then Jesus puts on Jack's coat.

Ask the group how does God now regard Jack? The answer is that God regards Jack as sinless and as his own son. It is as if Jack never did anything wrong. Ask how God now sees Jesus. The answer is that God sees Jesus as sinful. This according to the Bible is why Jesus had to die. Turn to **Isaiah 53.6** and ask someone to read it.

Then ask, "When Jesus died on the cross what happened to Jack's sins?" The answer is that those sins were attributed to Jesus. Jesus suffered death in Jack's place. Jesus took the penalty for Jack's sins. That is why Jesus had to die; death is the punishment for sin.

Then ask them to see something more. Look at **Romans 5.8** and ask "When did Jesus die for Jack?" The answer is that Jesus died for Jack while Jack was still a sinner – that is, while Jack was still busy with his sins. So ask, "If Jack never gives up his sins, if Jack never agrees to switch coats, would Jesus still have died?" The answer to this question is a resounding "Yes". The penalty for sin has already been paid by Jesus, and Jesus is now waiting for Jack to accept what he has done for him.

Look with the group at **Isaiah 59.2**. Ask, "What is my sin doing to my relationship with God?" The answer is that it is cutting you off from God – God is perfect and holy, so a sinful person cannot come into his presence.

Explain that when Jesus took your burden on the cross he experienced that separation from God which you should be experiencing, and that is why he cried out "My God, my God why have you forsaken me?" Look at **Matthew 27.46.**

Ask the group, "If Jesus has died for Jack, where does that leave Jack?" The answer is that Jack is free to come immediately into God's presence.

Key verse   (10 mins)

This week's key verse is **1 Peter 3.18:**
'For Christ also suffered for sins once for all, the righteous for the unrighteous, in order to bring you to God. He was put to death in the flesh, but made alive in the spirit.'

Learn the verse together in the usual way. Hand out blank cards so group members can write it out and put in their wallet or purse.

Make one further point about the cross. Say that there is one more question to address: 'Why couldn't God be like us?' When someone tells us that they are sorry and we judge them to be sincere, we forgive them readily. So why couldn't God do that? Why was it necessary for Jesus to suffer as he did? Ask them what they think, but say that the answer must lie in the nature of God – in who God is. Human anger against sin is appeased by a simple apology, but God's anger is not. For God, the only possible outcome of sin is death – even if that meant his own Son had to be the one who died.

3. The cross – a victory over evil   (20 mins)

Now explain that there is a third and final way of understanding the cross. Turn together to **Mark 1.21-27** and read it.

Explain that this is just one of several instances recorded in the gospels where Jesus is seen in victorious conflict with beings who are described as evil spirits or demons. Ask the group what they believe about evil spirits or forces. Do they have any personal experience of these things?

Look together at **Matthew 4.1-11**, where you will see the struggle between Jesus and the Devil. Point out that severe temptation to do wrong is an almost universal experience. This means that if people have ever experienced such temptation, they are already familiar with the Devil's activity in their own lives.

Now turn together to **Ephesians 6.11-12**, part of a letter written by St Paul to some Christians in Ephesus. It dates from about 30 years after the resurrection. In these verses Paul is encouraging Christians to see their lives as being like a fight or a war. This war is against the same spiritual forces that were ranged against Jesus.

Then turn with the group to **1 John 5.19** and see how powerful these spiritual forces are.

Explain that the battle between Jesus and the unseen forces rages on throughout the gospels and comes to a climax in **John 13.27-30**, when Satan entered into one of Jesus' own disciples. Judas betrayed Jesus, and this led directly to the crucifixion.

Now turn to **Colossians 2.15**. This verse says that the cross, far from being a victory for Satan, was actually a victory for Jesus, because by dying on the cross Jesus broke the power of evil. Ask people to get into groups of three or four, and ask them to discuss the question "In what sense was Satan's power broken on the cross?"

After a while bring them together to share their answers. In the discussion you could bring out the following points:

- The cross led directly to the resurrection of Jesus and the permanent defeat of the power of death.

- The cross led directly to the raising of Jesus to his place in heaven which gave him permanent authority over Satan (**Matthew 28.18**).

- The cross brings forgiveness for sin to all people who put their trust in Jesus. So Satan no longer has a basis to accuse Christians before God.

- The cross revealed the truth about God – that God is good, that he loves the people he has created, and that he has a plan to rescue them. So Satan is exposed as a liar (**John 8.44**) who accuses and oppresses people and tries to convince them that God does not really love them. The cross paved the way for continued victory for all Christians over Satan. **Ephesians 6** tells us how to obtain that victory.

Summary – the cross is an act of love   (10 mins)

Turn to the key verse from the last session, **John 3.16**. Remind the group what the verse says: the reason that God gave his Son to the world was because he loves people so much.

Ask the group to each think of someone they love very much, and then ask them what they would be prepared to do in order to demonstrate how much they love this person. Let them answer and then ask three questions:

- Would your love enable you to forgive this person no matter what they had done?

- Would your love mean that you would be prepared to suffer for this person if it meant that they would not have to suffer?

- If the person you love had an enemy would you be willing to expose yourself to a fight to the death against that enemy?

Then point out that Jesus did all of these things, and he did so because he really loves each one of us. He loves us because of who we are, because we are each created by God and made in the image of God. He knows all about us, our bad days and our good days, our strengths and our weaknesses, and yet he loves us. God is passionate about us; and that is why Jesus died.

Turn to **Philippians 2.8**. Jesus did not have to die. He died as an act of humble submission to his Father's will.

Beyond Ourselves

Session 6 : How to become a Christian

You have now reached the time when it will be your privilege to explain the message of the cross to your group. Do not be tempted to modify it in order to please your hearers; deliver it faithfully. The message of the cross is not human wisdom, and it will sometimes offend and puzzle people. But for those who receive it is the power of God. If you deliver a different message there will be no power and lives will not change.

Things you will need for this session :

- A large piece of paper or card with **Acts 2.38** written out.
- Bibles
- Small cards on which group members can write out the key verse.
- A whiteboard or flipchart.
- A bar of soap.
- A bowl of small presents

Introduction   (20 mins)

Open in prayer or with a time of silence. Then explain that the aims of this session are first that we should all understand what it means when someone says 'I am a Christian', and second that each of us should realise either that we already are Christians or that we are not yet there. Then there will be an opportunity for those who would like to take the step of becoming a Christian to do so by saying a prayer. Ask everyone to turn to this prayer, which is on page 40 in the coursebooks, and give them a minute to look at it. Explain that all who need to and wish to will be able to say this prayer at the end of the session.

Explain that there is no single verse in the Bible which says 'the definition of a Christian is ....' Instead we have to piece it together from a number of verses.

60

Say that the first verse we will look at is the key verse for this week, **Acts 2.38.** This is what Peter said on the very first occasion when some people asked the question "What do we have to do to become Christians?"

'Peter said to them, "Repent, and be baptized every one of you in the name of Jesus Christ so that your sins may be forgiven; and you will receive the gift of the Holy Spirit".'

Learn this verse together in the usual way and then hand out blank cards and ask everyone to write out the verse and put it in their wallet or purse.

Once the verse has been learned, ask the group to come up with a definition of a Christian, based just on this verse.

Then ask the group to turn to page 39 in their coursebooks where they will find a definition of a Christian taken from **Acts 2.38.** They will also find definitions based on each of the five key verses given so far.

Acts 2.38 – Christians are people who have repented and been baptised; their sins have been forgiven and they have received the Holy Spirit.

Psalm 23.6 – Christians are people who are experiencing God's love on a daily basis and are confident that this will go on forever.

Romans 6.23 – Christians are people who have received the gift of eternal life from Jesus although they have not earned it.

John 1.12 – Christians are people who have welcomed Jesus and who as a result have found that God has become a personal father.

John 3.16 – Christians are people who believe in Jesus and who, by believing, have received eternal life.

1 Peter 3.18 – Christians are people who have come to God having been set free from sin through the death of Jesus.

Put everyone into groups of three and ask each group to answer this question for each of the six verses: "If this is the definition of a Christian, am I a Christian, or do I still have some way to go?"

After a few minutes bring them back together again and ask, "From what you have seen from the six definitions, which of us is sure that we are Christians, which of us is sure we are not, and which of us are not sure?" Ask them to indicate briefly which of these best describes them. Make sure that those who are not there yet don't feel like failures – all of us are on a journey.

A Christian is someone who believes in Jesus   (20 mins)

Say that you now want to have a go at coming up with a simple definition of what a Christian is, based on these six verses. Say that your answer is in three parts; write it up on your board/flip chart as follows:

- A Christian is someone who believes in Jesus
- A Christian is someone who has received from Jesus
- A Christian is someone who has made a decision to follow Jesus.

Ask the group to look at this list, to sit for a moment and think how this applies to them. Can we each say that we believe in Jesus, and if not why not? Can we each say that we have received from Jesus, and if not would we like to? Can we each say that we have made a decision to follow Jesus, and if not can we say what is stopping us?

Say to the group that you would like to think about the first of these definitions – a Christian is someone who believes in Jesus. Ask what they think this means. What does it mean to believe in someone? Choose two people whom you know to be good friends, say Bethany and Katy. Ask Bethany "Would you say that you believe in Katy?" Bethany will say yes. Then ask her "When you say that you believe in Katy, what do you mean?" This should lead to a group discussion.

Explain that believing in Jesus includes believing certain things about him: Christians are people who believe particular things about Jesus to be true. Ask the group "What are these things? What are the things that all Christians believe about Jesus?"

Write their answers on your board/flipchart. Here are some of the things they may come up with:

- Jesus is the Son of God
- Jesus died for our sins
- Jesus conquered death
- Jesus has authority over all things
- Jesus gives his Holy Spirit to all who believe in him
- Jesus will one day return to the earth
- Jesus gives eternal life to all who ask him

Explain that these are the things that the Bible teaches about Jesus, which Jesus taught about himself, and which for 2,000 years Christians have believed to be true. Someone who does not believe these things cannot really say 'I am a Christian'. If anyone in the group realises that they do not yet believe them, they should be asking themselves 'Why not? These things are either true or untrue. Does not the weight of evidence suggest that they are far more likely to be true than untrue?'. We all need to make up our minds one way or the other.

A practical demonstration

Say to the group that when a Christian says that he believes in Jesus, he does not merely believe in the things we have written on the flipchart as a kind of creed which he says in church every week; he means that he has put his trust in these things. He is living his whole life on the basis that these things are true. Refer back to what Bethany said about Katy. When she says she believes in Katy, Bethany means that she trusts her. Illustrate this in the following way.

Before the meeting begins, place a bar of soap in your pocket (you will probably want to choose a wrapped bar!). Tell the group that there is a bar of soap in your pocket, and ask if they believe you. Some will think you are joking, so assure them that you are completely serious. You are trying to find out if they believe in you or not. So emphasize that when you say there is a bar of soap in your pocket you really do mean it. Now ask again if they believe that you are telling the truth. If anyone still doubts, press them until they all say that they do believe that there is a bar of soap in your pocket.

Now say that you want to see if they really believe. Will they live their lives on the assumption that the soap is really there? Ask them if they are prepared to put £10 on their belief? If the bar of soap turns out to really be there, they will get their £10 back plus a reward. But if it is not there, the £10 will be donated to charity.

Ask who will risk the £10 on their belief that there really is a bar of soap in your pocket? If they are unwilling to risk the £10, press them and pretend to be hurt: "You know me. You know that I tell the truth. There is a bar of soap in my pocket. Why won't you trust me? What kind of friendship can we have if you will not risk even £10 on what I have said being true?" Even if it takes some time, make sure that you get a commitment of £10 from all (or nearly all) of them.

Now raise the stakes – would they risk £100? Who is prepared to accept your word now? Keep on raising the stakes first to £1000, then even more and go on until you are asking people to stake everything they have on what you say being true. Some of the group will stick with you right to the end; some won't.

Now produce the bar of soap and explain the illustration. Tell them that you know that you are not Jesus, and you understand therefore if they find it hard to trust you. The illustration however is a simple way of showing what it means to trust Jesus. The things which you listed together on the flipchart as being true about Jesus are indeed true – there is strong evidence to support them – but no one can completely prove them. Jesus asks us to take his word for it, just as in the illustration you asked them to take your word for the soap. The reason you kept pressing them is to show that Jesus wants us to stake everything on his word being true.

Now place a bowl of small presents in the middle of the room – wrapped chocolates, chewy bars, or fruit. Make sure that you have more presents than there are people in the group; and have a variety so that there is bound to be something that will appeal to everyone.

Say to the group that you promised a reward to anyone who would trust you when you said that you had a bar of soap in your pocket. These gifts are the reward. Encourage everyone to take a gift, unwrap it and eat it. Say that if anyone refused to believe you then strictly speaking they should not get a present – but that you want them each to have one anyway.

Then say to them: "If you decide to believe what I say, all you will get is a chocolate. But if you decide to believe Jesus, he will give you amazing rewards." Ask the people who have said that they are sure that they are Christians what rewards they have already received from Jesus.

A Christian is a person who has received from Jesus (10 mins)

Now say that this brings you on to the second definition of a Christian: a Christian is someone who has received from Jesus.

Refer back to page 39 in the coursebooks, and the six definitions of a Christian. Ask the group to look at these definitions and answer the question "What is it, according to these 6 verses, that all Christians have received from Jesus?" Write their answers on the flipchart. You should get something like this:

- **The fatherhood of God** - we experience the love of God on a daily basis – it is as if God has become our personal Father.

- **Forgiveness** – we are set free from our past – all our sins and failings are completely forgiven and forgotten by God.

- **The Holy Spirit** - we have received the gift of the Holy Spirit. The Holy Spirit is the presence of God in us and with us.

- **Eternal life** – our experience of life in God will not end when we die. Our new relationship with God will last beyond death into eternity.

Say that when we come to the prayer at the end of the session, these are the things that we will ask for. Explain that you yourself once asked God to give you these four things, and he did. As a result you now have a relationship with God in which he is your loving, caring, disciplining Father; you have the inner peace which comes from knowing you are forgiven; you have experienced the power of God working in you which comes from the presence of the Holy Spirit; and you are filled with joy and hope as you look forward to the time when you will see Jesus face to face. Say that every true Christian you have ever known shares this experience, and that this has been so right back to biblical times; if anyone prays today you are confident that these things will be given to them too.

Now say to the group that in life some of things are earned by us and some are given to us. Can they suggest some simple examples?

Then look together at **Ephesians 2.8-9**, which says that our salvation is a gift. All the things which we have listed on the flipchart are gifts. We can do nothing to earn them; all we can do is receive them. Remind the group that you have just given them each a small gift, and ask them what they needed to do to receive that gift? The answer is that they needed to believe. Then say that it is exactly the same with all the things you listed. They are all gifts, things which we could never earn. All we have to do to receive them is to believe. If we put our trust in Jesus, God always responds.

Remind the group of what happened two sessions earlier when you fell backwards and a member of the group caught you. By falling
66

backwards you declared your trust in that person, and your trust was rewarded. It is exactly the same when we put our trust in Jesus.

A Christian is a person who has made a decision (20 mins)

Now explain that this brings you to the third definition of a Christian: a Christian is someone who has made a decision to follow Jesus.

Refer the group to page 39 of the coursebooks, where they will find the following verses:

> Mark 1.15, Matthew 4.19, Acts 2.38,
> Luke 14.26-27, Matthew 13.44, Matthew 7.13-14

Put them into small groups to consider these verses. Each verse describes a decision which all who are Christians have made. Ask them to identify what that decision is. After a few minutes, call them back together to pool their answers.

Probably the best single word to describe this decision is 'repentance'. The word 'repent' literally means 'to rethink'. When we make a decision to become a Christian we are deciding to think again about the way we look at everything. Share with the group what this has meant for you. How have your priorities changed? How has your behaviour changed? Ask those who are sure that they are already Christians what repentance has meant for them.

Then say that positively, repentance means making Jesus the centre of our lives, worshipping him, following him, living by his priorities, and working unashamedly for his cause. He becomes the new priority and benchmark for all we do.

Use **Matthew 4.19** to illustrate this, making the following points:

Peter was a fisherman; fishing was his whole life. There is nothing wrong with being a fisherman, but Jesus was calling him to something altogether new. It was not that Peter would never go fishing again, but rather that fishing would no longer be what his life was all about. Every Christian who has ever lived has felt the same. People become Christians because they want their lives to take a new direction – the direction that Jesus determines.

Then negatively, repentance means turning away from anything that is wrong, for example any kind of dishonesty or immorality. But it also includes giving up non-Christian or sub-Christian religious practices such as consulting mediums or involvement in freemasonry.

Explain that the decision to become a Christian is always a big one because it means a loss of freedom. It means changing from living in a way that you have chosen (not necessarily a bad way, but not a Christian way) to living in the way that Jesus taught.

Put people back in their groups and ask them to share what they think would be the biggest challenge for them if they were to make a decision to follow Jesus today.

A prayer of commitment (20 mins)

Bring them together again and allow them to ask questions. Then say that today you have looked in some detail together at what is involved in becoming and being a Christian. Now it is time to actually do it! Ask them to turn again to the prayer on page 40 in their coursebooks. Explain that you are going to say this prayer, and that if they are ready you would like them to say it with you.

Explain that it is entirely up to them whether or not they pray this prayer. Indeed, if they are not ready, they should not pray it – there will be another opportunity later. But if God has been speaking to them while they have been doing the course, and if they can see no reason why they should not turn to Jesus now, then urge them to join in the prayer. Through the prayer they will be saying to God that today they have made a solemn choice, the choice to regard themselves as a follower of Jesus, and to live by trusting him and by adopting his values. Say that those who are already sure that they are Christians will not need to say the prayer again; those who are unsure should definitely say the prayer because it will be a moment to look back to. When someone asks "Are you a Christian?", they will be able to say "Yes; I made a definite decision on that particular day."

Explain that this is a serious step and that you are sure they have already been thinking about it carefully. But it would be good for you all to pause for a moment now so that everyone can think for themselves whether they want to say the prayer.

Ask them to be quiet, to close their eyes and to consider three questions. Ask the questions one at a time, pausing after each one to give them a chance to think:

1. "The first question is this: Do you believe in Jesus? I do not mean that you have no doubts at all, but as you have looked at the evidence about Jesus are you persuaded? Can you say 'Yes, Jesus, I believe you are from God, and that you have the answers to the world's needs and to my needs?' And are you prepared to put your trust in him?"

2. "The second question is this: Are you ready to change the way that you live? Will you follow Jesus to the best of your ability? Will you turn away from anything that you know to be wrong?"

3. "The third question is this: Are you ready to receive from him? He promises to forgive you. He promises to fill you with the presence and power of His Holy Spirit. He promises not to forget you when you die but to welcome you. He promises to become your personal father and to be there for you every day. Are you ready to open your heart and receive forgiveness for all that has passed and new life for all that is to come?"

Now ask them to open their eyes and read the prayer which you are about to say. Explain that you will say it sentence by sentence, and that you would like them to repeat the sentences after you.

It is often best to find out who wants to say the prayer, and then to invite them to pray aloud. If you decide to do it this way, go afterwards to each one who has prayed and pray for them individually.

But sometimes it is better to ask people to pray quietly in their hearts. If you decide to do it this way, then say the prayer aloud but pause after each sentence so that they can offer their own prayers in the silences.

If you do it this way you will not know who has prayed and who has not, so you will have to ask those who have prayed to let you know. If they tell you that they have prayed, you can then offer to pray for them individually.

If anyone does say the prayer, look briefly with them before they go home at exercise 1 in the member's coursebook (page 40).

You will see that this exercise suggests that they set aside 15 minutes each day to read the Bible and pray. Explain briefly why they will find it helpful to do this, and then offer to do it with them the first time so that you can show them how it works for you. If they would like you to do this, discuss with them when and where you will meet. The best options are:

- Do it on the very next day if at all possible.

- Go to their home if at all possible. You are trying to establish them in a habit, the habit of a daily time of quiet with God. If you go just once to their territory you will find that they gain the motivation to keep up the habit for themselves. You won't need to do it twice.

- Choose the earliest possible time in the day. Ask them what time they normally get up in the morning and suggest that you turn up at that time or a little earlier.

Note: If anyone does pray in this way you may find it helpful to give them a copy of Decision, a short and inexpensive booklet designed for those who are new to faith. See p 8.

Beyond Ourselves

Session 7: The Holy Spirit

Things you will need for this session :

- A large piece of paper or card with **Luke 11.13** written out
- Bibles
- Small cards on which group members can write out the key verse.
- Whiteboard or flipchart.
- Pens & paper

Introduction   (10 mins)

Open with prayer or with a time of silence.

Explain that in both this and the next session you will be thinking about the Holy Spirit.

Begin by reviewing last week's memory verse, **Acts 2.38**. Ask if someone in the group is able to recite the verse from memory and then tell you in their own words what it says about the Holy Spirit. The answer is that if we repent (that is, if we make a decision to change the direction of our life and follow Jesus with all our heart) then Jesus will give us the gift of the Holy Spirit.

Explain that in the Bible God is spoken of in three ways:

- First God the Father, the creator of everything, the one to whom Jesus prayed
- Secondly God the Son, that is Jesus
- Thirdly God the Holy Spirit. The Holy Spirit is God living in us and becoming active through us.

When we say that Jesus will give us his Holy Spirit, we mean that the Spirit of God, that is God himself, will come to us.

Remind the group that last week some of them said a prayer of commitment to Jesus, asking him to send the Holy Spirit to them. Those who said this prayer should already have direct experience of the presence of the Holy Spirit in their lives. Ask if anyone has anything they would like to share, or if they have any questions?

Explain that, because the presence of the Spirit is the mark of an authentic Christian, you want to be sure that everyone in the group has received the Spirit. So in this session and the next there will be further opportunities to pray for this amazing gift.

Key verse   (10 mins)

This week's key verse is **Luke 11.13**:

'If you then, who are evil, know how to give good gifts to your children, how much more will the heavenly Father give the Holy Spirit to those who ask him!'

Take a few minutes to learn this verse together, then hand out cards so people can write it out for meditation during the week.

Point out that:

- Like Jesus, the Holy Spirit is God
- Like Jesus, the Holy Spirit comes from heaven
- Like Jesus, the Holy Spirit lives among us here on earth
- But, unlike Jesus, the Holy Spirit has no bodily form. The Holy Spirit is able to be everywhere at once; today the Holy Spirit is at work in every country on earth, and is especially present whenever any group of Christians meet together in submission to God.

Now pray and invite the Holy Spirit to be present in today's session.

The Holy Spirit in the Old and New Testaments
(20 mins)

Explain to the group that you plan now to do some Bible study on the subject of the Holy Spirit. Tell them that they will find the verses you plan to look at on page 46 of the coursebooks.

Look first at **Deuteronomy 34.9.** Ask someone to read it. Explain that in the Old Testament the Holy Spirit was not available to everyone but only to special people. Joshua was one of these special people. How do they think Joshua received the Holy Spirit?

Help them to see that Joshua received the Spirit when Moses laid hands on him. Turn together to **Acts 9.17**, and show that Paul also received the Spirit by the laying on of hands. Look at verses 18 and 19 and ask the group what happened when the Spirit came upon Paul?

Go back to **Deuteronomy 34.9** and ask: "When Joshua received the Spirit, what was it that the Spirit brought to him?" The answer is that Joshua received wisdom. Explain that this did not mean that Joshua became clever! It meant that from that moment on, Joshua always knew what to do next – because the Spirit told him. This is an essential gift for a spiritual leader. Anyone in a position of leadership needs to know what to do next. Instead of relying on his or her natural abilities, every spiritual leader has to learn to rely on the Spirit's voice. The Spirit makes possible what otherwise would be impossible.

Joshua is described as being full of the Spirit. This means that everyone could see the Spirit's presence in his life. Ask if anyone is familiar with the story of Joshua – do they know what happened through him? Explain to them how by the Spirit's power Joshua led the people of God through the River Jordan and into victory over the city of Jericho. Both of these events depended on supernatural power, and they are typical of what happened in the Old Testament whenever the Spirit came on a person chosen by God for a particular task.

Ask the group if they can think of other biblical characters who were also filled with the Spirit. Examples are Elijah, Elisha, Samuel, Samson, Gideon, John the Baptist, Jesus himself, and others. All these people were able to do amazing things by the power of the Holy Spirit.

Explain that if we have the Spirit, like Joshua, we too will find that we are given power to accomplish everything that God gives us to do – sometimes quite amazing power. For example, Jesus is not here to pray directly for the sick, but we are here and we can pray in his name. This power comes only from the Spirit. Give examples from your own experience.

Now read **Matthew 3.16**. This verse describes how Jesus received the Spirit. It shows that he belonged to the long line of Spirit-filled special people which the Old Testament describes.

Then look at **Matthew 12.28** and ask the group what Jesus was able to do because of the power of the Spirit within him? Explain that everything that Jesus did which we call miraculous was done in the same way. The Holy Spirit acted more powerfully through Jesus than he had ever done through anyone before.

Now turn with the group to **Joel 2.28-29**. Explain that this prophecy is important because it says that the Holy Spirit will one day come upon 'all flesh'. This means that the Holy Spirit will no longer be restricted to special people, but will be available to ordinary people like ourselves. This prophecy remained unfulfilled until Jesus came, 500 years after Joel.

Finally, turn to **John 7.37-39.** Explain that John is describing how Jesus went to Jerusalem to attend the annual festival known as the Feast of Booths. At this festival the Jewish nation would gather both to remember their history and also to look forward to the time when Joel's prophecy would be fulfilled.

At the heart of the festival was a procession which happened every day and ended with the pouring out of water in the temple. As the water was poured out, the people in Jerusalem looked back to the time when their forefathers ran out of water in the wilderness. Moses had struck a rock, and water had poured out of it. It was a great miracle of God. The people were reminding themselves that God will always provide water when it is needed.

But as well as looking back to Moses' miracle the people used this ceremony to look forward to another miracle day – the day when Joel's prophecy would be fulfilled and the water of the Spirit would be poured out on all flesh including, they hoped, themselves.

John records that Jesus interrupted this temple ceremony at its climax. He spoke in a very loud voice, and his interruption must have been very dramatic. What he said is recorded for us in John 7.

Look together at the verses and then ask the group what Jesus said about the coming of the Spirit. It is very important that they understand that Jesus promised that the Spirit would be given to **all** who came to him. Jesus is the source of the Spirit. Ask what will happen to us if we too come to Jesus and ask for the gift of the Spirit? The answer is that the Spirit will pour not just *into* us but also, just as the water flowed from the rock, out *from* us. We too will be able to hear God's voice and we too will have supernatural power to one degree or another.

The disciples receive the Spirit and the first church is born (20 mins)

Turn together to **Acts 2.1-4**. Explain that this chapter describes the

fulfilment both of what Joel had promised 500 years earlier, and of what Jesus had promised in John chapter 7.

Tell the group that, in New Testament times, the Jews held several annual festivals, all of them in Jerusalem. The Feast of Booths, where the water was poured out, was just one of them. Sometime later there was a second festival in Jerusalem, the Feast of Passover. During this festival Jesus was arrested, tried, and crucified.

After another six weeks it was time for a third festival. This was a one day event, similar to the harvest festival which is common today; it was called the Feast of Pentecost. And it was on this day that the Holy Spirit first came upon those who believed in Jesus.

Tell them that the first believers were a group of 120 people, all of whom had seen Jesus alive after he had been put to death on the cross. Jesus had told this group that they were to pray together and wait for the coming of the Spirit. **Acts 2.1-4** describes what happened when the Spirit came. Read it together.

Look together at the verses, and help the group to identify how the disciples knew that the Spirit had indeed come upon them.

- They heard the sound of a wind

- They saw tongues of fire

- They were able to communicate with the people in Jerusalem in their native languages although they themselves could not speak these languages.

Explain to the group that these manifestations of the Spirit's presence do happen occasionally today, but that the things that happen are not normally as overwhelming as this. It was a case of something very special for a very special occasion. (The gift of tongues is common among Christians today, but is more commonly given as a spiritual language for prayer or prophecy, and only occasionally as a miracle which enables someone to speak in a language which is not their own).

Continuing the story, explain that after the Spirit came upon the disciples Peter spoke to the crowd who had gathered for the festival. Look at **Acts 2.37** together, and ask what impact Peter's sermon had? The answer is that many people were 'cut to the heart', presumably because they realised that by calling for the death of Jesus they had crucified the Son of God.

These people then asked Peter what they should do. As you have learned in the key verse, Peter told them to repent of their sins and to be baptised.

Now turn to **Acts 2.41**. 3000 people did repent and were baptised, and then the gift of the Spirit came upon them. **Acts 2.42-47** describes what happened.

Ask the group to read the verses and tell you what this community of 3000 people was like after the Holy Spirit had come. Let them answer and write the answers on your board/flipchart as follows:

First there was much evidence of the supernatural:

1. God was clearly at work among them

Secondly there was among the people a spirit of devotion or commitment.

2. They loved the apostles' teaching (for us this means the New Testament)
3. They loved meeting together in fellowship
4. They loved to pray together
5. They loved to share bread and wine (for us this means the Sacraments)

And finally at a human level they were a most attractive community.

6. They were a community at ease with itself
7. They displayed great generosity and sacrifice
8. They were constantly and enthusiastically praising God
9. New Christians were being added all the time

Explain that all these things are still found today whenever the Holy Spirit comes into a community of people. If we pray for the Holy Spirit and the Holy Spirit comes to us, our community, our small group, will begin to resemble that first Christian community in Jerusalem.

You should find that the session still has about half an hour to run, and at this point you will have to make a decision. The three sections which follow are all optional, and you will probably not have time for all three. The first section 'Prayer for our group' is one you will probably want to include and should be left out only if you are sure you want to include both the other sections, 'Asking for the gifts of the Holy Spirit' and 'Expelling evil spirits'. But even this first section should be attempted only if you are fairly confident that all the group members are now in a position to participate positively in a time of prayer.

If you decide to leave out all the remaining sections it can only be because several of your group members have not yet reached the point where they believe in Jesus and have committed themselves to him. If you think this is the case then say to the group that next time you will be offering to pray for each member of the group that they may personally receive the Holy Spirit. Point out that the Holy Spirit is given to believers, and that because of this you would like the group to do an exercise on becoming a believer. This is the exercise:

Give each member of the group a piece of paper and a pen. Ask them to draw a line down the middle of the piece of paper and to write two headings. The first heading is 'Reasons to believe in Jesus', and the second heading is 'Reasons not to believe in Jesus'.

Then ask them to draw a horizontal line at the bottom of the page and put a heading 'My decision is.' In this space they should either write 'To become a believer', or 'To decide against believing', or 'I believe the following questions to be critical to my decision.'

Ask everyone in the group to fill up the piece of paper and then to share their answers with the group.

Prayer for the group   (15 mins)

If you decide to go ahead with this section refer to
the list of nine items on your flipchart. Say that
none of these things can happen through our own
efforts. They will be ours only if the Holy Spirit
comes among us and gives them to us. For example
we could probably stir ourselves up to seem
devoted to prayer, but without the inner motivation
that the Spirit can give us, this devotion will be very
short lived. The Spirit knows how to make prayer so
rewarding that we will want to pray.

Remind them of the key verse for this week. Jesus said that if we lack
the Holy Spirit all we need do is ask – so that is what you are going to
do now. Invite each member of the group to take responsibility for one
of the nine items. Begin by asking who would like to pray that it will
become obvious that God is at work among us, and finish by asking
who would like to pray that our friends would come to faith in Jesus.
Then pray together, asking for all nine things to be given to you. As you
pray together, join hands. Explain that joining hands is a symbol of your
unity as together you ask the Spirit to bestow his gifts upon your
group.

Before you pray explain that prayer is simply us opening our mouths
and speaking to God. There is no need to try to find special words –
when we pray, we just talk to God naturally. Explain that as we make
the effort to do this, we find that the Holy Spirit comes and helps us to
pray. Begin the prayer time by asking, as the leader, for the Spirit's
help; and then pray one by one for each of the nine items.

Asking for the gifts of the Holy Spirit   (15 mins)

Include this section only if you feel the group is ready for it. In the
previous section you asked the Spirit to bestow his gifts on the group
as a whole. Now you will ask the Spirit to give things to the group

members as individuals.

Turn with the group to page 53 in the coursebooks, where you will find a list of the things that the Holy Spirit sometimes brings to a person's life when he comes. Emphasise to the group that no one receives all of these things but that, between you, you can expect to receive some if not most of them.

Ask them to each choose one item from the list that they would personally love to have if the Holy Spirit in his grace would give it to them. Ask everyone to share what this is, but allow people to pass if they feel unsure.

Then ask those who have shared if it would be okay for you to pray for them as Ananias prayed for Paul. Move around the room laying hands on the heads or the shoulders of each person who would like you to, and ask for that particular gift to be given to them. Then ask some of them to pray in the same way for you.

Expelling evil spirits   (15 mins)

Omit this section if after praying you feel that some in the group are not ready for it.

Explain that if we want a holy God to make his home in us it is wise to get rid of the unholy things that we have, either knowingly or unknowingly, given space to in our lives.

Read **Luke 4.31-37**. This is an example of the authoritative way that Jesus dealt with evil spirits. His aim was to bring wholeness and peace. Explain that evil spirits can still oppress us today. No one is completely sure why this is, but there is much evidence that the presence of evil spirits is a result of a person getting involved in one way or another with what the Ten Commandments called 'idol worship', and which today is broadly called the 'occult' – this includes such things as astrology, fortune telling, witchcraft, black magic, séances, ouija boards, spirit-mediums and freemasonry. Much of this is outlawed in Deuteronomy 18.

It also seems probable that evil spirits can be inherited from family members who were themselves involved in these things. And it is even possible that they could have been introduced through items in our homes (eg holiday souvenirs – amulets, charms, sculptures) that have links with other 'gods' or spirits from Eastern or traditional tribal religions.

Explain that some people may be troubled by:

- a sense of oppression
- irrational/intense fears
- inability to concentrate on Bible reading, or on sermons (perhaps they always seem to nod off, or their mind to wander).

All these may indicate the influence of evil spirits.

Ask if there is anyone present who has been involved with the occult or who thinks they may be troubled by evil spirits. If no one responds, just say that that is good, but ask anyone who has second thoughts to let you know. The presence of evil spirits is more common than most people realise, and they often mess up our lives.

If some do acknowledge an involvement with the occult, or feel that they have any of the symptoms, then explain that Jesus gave his disciples the authority to drive out evil spirits, and that you can pray a simple prayer together to make sure that this has been done. There is a possibility that at this point an evil spirit will make its presence obvious. If this happens (it probably won't), do not panic but simply follow the procedure outlined below. This prayer will restore calm to the situation.

- Begin by inviting the Holy Spirit to be present.

- Pray the Lord's Prayer together, asking each person to think as they pray of any activities in their own lives or those of close family members which may have opened a door to evil.
- When you have finished the Lord's Prayer, pray a prayer thanking God for sending Jesus to defeat the powers of evil. Claim his protection on all present.

- Command any evil spirits to go in the name of Jesus. If an evil spirit is obviously present, insist that it goes to another place and keep on insisting until it does go.

- Invite the Holy Spirit to cleanse and fill each person present.

If there is anyone in the group who feels they need a longer time of prayer, you should arrange to see them on a separate occasion, or refer them to someone else. Such prayer should only be undertaken with the authority of a church leader, and by two people who have experience in this ministry.

Beyond Ourselves

Session 8 : Receiving the Spirit

There is a lot of material in this session. With care you should be able to include it all, but the most important section is the last, so don't allow the timing to lag so that you either leave the last section out or send people home too late.

Things you will need for this session :

- A large piece of paper or card with **John 7.37-39** written out
- Bibles
- Small cards on which group members can write out the key verse
- A second card with **Ephesians 1.13-14** written out.
- A recording of the song 'This is the air I breathe' by Michael W Smith

---

Introduction and key verse   (7 mins)

Begin with this week's key verse, **John 7.37-39**:

'Let anyone who is thirsty come to me, and let the one who believes in me drink. As the scripture has said, "Out of the believer's heart shall flow rivers of living water." Now he said this about the Spirit, which believers in him were to receive.

Learn it together, then hand out blank cards for people to write it out and put it in their purse or wallet.

Then lead the group in prayer – come together before Jesus, express your shared faith in him, and ask that today he would fill you afresh with his Holy Spirit.

The guarantee   (10 mins)

Refer to the card with the following verses written out, or if you prefer write up these verses on your flipchart.

Ephesians 1.13-14: And you also were included in Christ when you heard the message of truth, the gospel of your salvation. When you believed, you were marked in him with a seal, the promised Holy Spirit, who is a deposit guaranteeing our inheritance until the redemption of those who are God's possession – to the praise of his glory. (NB this is the NIV translation)

Explain that these verses are important, but that it can be quite difficult to get your mind round them. So ask the group to sit in silence and work out what they are saying. Then ask them a number of questions:

1. In these verses who was it who received the gift of the Spirit?

Explain that Paul is writing to a group of recent converts who lived in Ephesus. These people had heard the gospel, the good news about Jesus. Because Jesus had died on the cross their sins had been forgiven. Because Jesus was raised to life they themselves had received the gift of eternal life. These people had believed this, and God had sent his Holy Spirit upon them – just as the key verse from John 7 says he will. The Holy Spirit is given to those who believe in Jesus.

2. The Holy Spirit was given in order to guarantee something. What is it that is being guaranteed?

The answer is that it is our inheritance that is being guaranteed.

3. What is our inheritance? What is it that all Christians will one day inherit? What are we all looking forward to?

The answer is that, although we have a great deal to look forward to in this life, what is meant here is our final inheritance. God promises that one day we shall enjoy a new life in eternity with him. Something unimaginably wonderful is being stored up for us, something beyond our wildest dreams.

4. How do Christians know that they will one day receive this inheritance?

We know this because we have received the guarantee – that is, we know because we have received the Holy Spirit.

Illustrating the principle of the guarantee

Illustrate this in one of two ways, depending on the composition of the group.

Perhaps someone in the group is wearing an engagement ring and another person a wedding ring. Point out that an engagement ring is given as a guarantee of the wedding ring. Christians are like people who are wearing an engagement ring as they wait for the day of their wedding. The Holy Spirit is the engagement ring. The wedding comes after we die and we enter into heaven to live forever in a blissful union with Jesus.

Alternatively, ask if anyone in the group has ever made a down payment. A down payment is when you say to someone 'I will pay you so much today and the rest later.' The down payment is considerable, but it is not the whole amount. The point of the down payment is that it guarantees the rest. The Holy Spirit is the down payment and our life in glory with God is the rest that is to come. The Holy Spirit is the guarantee of eternal life.

To be a guarantee the Holy Spirit must be more than a concept; he must be more than a theoretical idea or a religious ceremony. Rather the Holy Spirit is a tangible experience of God in our lives. God sends the Holy Spirit as his way of saying 'I love you, you are mine, and I will never abandon you.'

Tangible evidence – A relationship with God   (18 mins)

This leads on to a further question. Explain that at the end of the session today you will be saying prayers asking for the Holy Spirit to be given to the group just as he was to the Christians in Ephesus. The question is, 'how will we know that we have received the Spirit?'

Turn together to **John 3.8**, where Jesus says that the Holy Spirit is like the wind. Point out that if we go outside on a windy day, it is hard to say where the wind is coming from or where it is going. But we can easily tell that the wind is there. In the same way when the Spirit comes, we can tell that the Spirit is there.

Ask for a volunteer, explaining that you need someone who is quite clear that they believe in Jesus and that they have decided to follow Jesus. Suppose the volunteer's name is Bill.

Say to the group that Bill is quite obviously a believer in Jesus and so, assuming that Bill is willing, at the end of the session you will be praying for Bill that he will receive the gift of the Holy Spirit, just as Jesus said he would. Or, if Bill has already received this guarantee, you will be praying that the Spirit will make himself known to Bill in even clearer ways.

Ask the group "When the Holy Spirit comes to Bill, how do you think he will make his presence felt? How will Bill know that he has received the Spirit?"

Let them answer, but say that one thing that will definitely happen is that Bill will find that from today he will enter into a new relationship with God. Turn with the group to page 53 in their coursebooks, where they will find the words of a song. Explain that this song, *This is the air I breathe*, is a typical Christian song written by someone who knows what it is like to have the Holy Spirit living in him. Play the song to them. While the music is playing ask them to look at the words. When the music stops ask them to say how they think the writer of this song is experiencing the Spirit.

Now explain that when you pray for Bill you will be asking that the Holy Spirit will give him the same kind of experience that is being enjoyed by the writer of the song.

Ask if anyone in the group has ever fallen in love. If anyone says yes, ask them to describe what that experience was like. Then say that being filled with the Holy Spirit is like falling in love with God. It's the beginning of something new and exciting, something rewarding and life-changing.

Turn together to **Romans 5.5** for a description of what happens when the Spirit comes. This experience of falling in love with God is something that will happen to us again and again throughout our lives. A love relationship with God is very similar to a love relationship between people. It begins with an initial falling in love – this is when the Spirit comes for the first time. At times, as in human relationships, the relationship with God becomes more routine and less emotional, but then something happens and we fall in love with God again as the Spirit fills our hearts.

You may find that someone in the group will say "I believe in God but I don't think I have ever fallen in love with him." If so, respond gently, explaining that this is something we will be praying later on will happen to all of us. The Spirit is not given so that we will have a dry faith with our emotions unaffected.

Say that falling in love is one way of explaining the relationship we have with God when the Spirit comes. Another way to describe the relationship can be found in **Galatians 4.6-7**. Turn to these verses and ask the group how our new relationship with God is described? When the Holy Spirit comes

God becomes our Father and we are like children to him, members of his family.

Ask the group to each share one thing which they really valued in their human father. When everyone has shared, say that God is like all of that and more. Share your own testimony of how you have experienced God as Father, and explain that it is because you have God as your Father that you know that you have the Spirit, and because you have the Spirit that you know that God will always be your Father.

There may be some in the group who have had only bad experiences of their human father. If so assure them that God will be different and will more than replace the father that they never had.

Tangible evidence – being changed   (15 mins)

Now explain that another thing that will happen to Bill when the Spirit comes is that the Spirit will help him to change. Indeed the Spirit will *cause* him to change.

Turn together to **Galatians 5.19-21**, and ask someone to read it. Explain that this is a list of things that are often found in the lives of people who do not have the Spirit. Write the list on your flipchart.

Now look together at **Galatians 5.22-23**. Explain that this is a list of the things that are always found in the lives of people who have received the Spirit. Write this list on your flipchart alongside the other list.

Ask if anyone can think of someone – not a parent – who came into their life and influenced them in a big way, so that they can truly say "I am a better person today because I have known this person." Then explain that this is exactly how the Holy Spirit works. He comes into our lives as an influence. If any of the things on the first list are true of Bill, then under the Spirit's influence they will gradually disappear from his life; and if any of the things in the second list are not true of Bill, they will gradually appear in his life.

Explain that spiritual growth is similar to physical growth. We have all seen a baby or toddler growing taller and stronger, and the same is true of spiritual growth. Spiritual birth is not the end of the Holy Spirit's work in us – it is just the start. When we receive the gift of the Holy Spirit, we receive the power or potential to develop according to a new pattern. We become more and more like Jesus.

Summarise: When the Spirit comes it is like falling in love with God. It is like acquiring a wonderful new father. It is like entering into a relationship with someone who will be a good influence in your life.

Tangible evidence – words   (10 mins)

Then say that there is something else that the Spirit will bring to Bill. When the Spirit comes to Bill he will find that again and again he is able to hear the voice of God. This will especially happen to him when he reads his Bible. But Bill will hear the voice of God in many other ways as well.

Turn together to **1 Corinthians 2.11-12** and ask someone to read it. Ask the group how we as Christians are going to know the thoughts of God. The answer is that we will know when the Spirit speaks those thoughts to us. Ask if anyone in the group who has had this experience of knowing that they are being spoken to by God. Allow people to share and be ready to share yourself.

Tangible evidence – the Spirit in the church   (10 mins)

Then say that finally when the Spirit comes we will find that he draws us together into a new community. It is not just that the Spirit is in Bill and in you but that the Spirit is in all of us – the Spirit is in the community.

Turn to **Acts 2.41-47.** Remind the group that we looked at this passage last time, when we used it to identify nine things that we can expect to happen to our group when the Holy Spirit comes to us. Can they remember what they were? Remind them:

- God will clearly and unmistakeably be at work amongst us.
- We will fall in love with the Bible.
- We will be devoted to one another and love to be together.
- We will love to pray together.
- We will be devoted to the sacraments, sharing bread and wine together.
- We will become a community at ease with itself.
- There will be great generosity and sacrifice amongst us.
- We will love to spend time together singing and praising God
- New Christians will often join us.

These things will not happen unless the Holy Spirit makes them happen. Say that when these things start to happen then you will know that you have the Holy Spirit.

If you have time, turn to **1 Corinthians 12.4-11** and read it together.

This passage describes what happens when Christians who have the Holy Spirit pray together. Encourage the group by saying that we will find that this happens to us too if we pray together. The Holy Spirit makes this happen.

Explain that different people have different roles in prayer. Some people will find that as you pray together they are given a desire to pray for those who are unwell, and that their prayer is powerful. Some will find that as you pray God speaks to them through what Paul calls a word of prophecy or knowledge or wisdom. And some will find that like the early apostles they receive the gift of tongues. As you explain this, illustrate from your own experience, and encourage group members to share too.

So when the Spirit comes to Bill he will find that he begins to enjoy prayer. As he prays with the rest of the group he may discover that the Spirit has given him the gift of tongues, or he may find that he has a gift of healing, or that he is able to hear what God is saying to the group.

If you found time in the last session for the section on page 79 'Asking for the gifts of the Holy Spirit' remind the group that last time some of us shared what was the particular gift we most desired. When the Spirit comes to Bill he may well find that this wish has been granted.

Praying for the Holy Spirit to come   (20 mins)

Explain that it is time now to pray together for the Holy Spirit to come, not only to Bill but to all of us.

Say that some people may still feel that they are not yet ready for this, and reassure them that anyone who feel like this should remain seated and quietly pray for the others. Then ask those who want to be prayed for to stand.

Explain to those who are standing that before we pray for the Spirit we must first express our faith in Jesus and our decision to turn from everything that is wrong in our lives and to follow him. Say that we can do this by using the words traditionally used in the Church of England baptism service.

- I turn to Christ
- I renounce evil
- I repent of my sins (they may want to name specific issues)

Allow a short time for reflection and then, when they are ready, ask each member of the group in turn to say these words. You as leader should say them too.

When each of you has said the words, turn to **Revelation 3.20** and read it out to the group:

'Listen! I am standing at the door, knocking; if you hear my voice and open the door, I will come in to you and eat with you, and you with me.'

Explain that this is the Holy Spirit speaking. The Spirit promises to come and live in each person who opens their hearts to him. He will also come into the group as a whole and live there too.

Point out that this is extremely good news: it is amazing that the Spirit of God who is himself the creator of the entire universe is willing to come to us! This is a gift, it is free, and it is undeserved. When the Spirit comes we can look forward to depending on him every day for the rest of our lives.

Say that you will ask each of them to pray in their own words, asking for the gift of the Spirit, and that after each has prayed you would like them to remain standing so that you can pray for them one by one. Explain that, unless they ask you not to, you will lay hands on them. And now ask them to pray in turn.

After each person has prayed ask them to remain standing and to wait. Suggest that they simply open themselves to receive whatever he has for them. What happens next depends on God and not on them.

Keep your own eyes open and watch. Pray that you may be allowed to keep in step with what God is doing, and do not be in a hurry. Pray for each person but in no particular order. Always ask God who you should pray for next. Do not pray using a formula; listen to God. You may be given a different form of words for each one. When you pray, lay your hands gently on their head or shoulders.

You should expect each person being prayed for to experience the presence of God in one way or another. (This is quite scary for the person praying, but put your trust in God and go ahead. Unless you have faith in what is happening it will be very difficult for them to have faith). Move around the group, laying hands on each person in turn and praying.

Sometimes this kind of exposure to the Holy Spirit will cause someone to feel unsteady or even to fall. Be aware of this possibility and make sure that you or someone else is in a position to catch them if they do. If someone does fall do not be alarmed; just allow them to rest.

Finally you too should pray the prayer based on Revelation 3.20 and then ask the group to lay hands on you and pray that you too will be filled by the Holy Spirit.

When the praying is finished, ask people to share how it felt. If there is someone for whom nothing much has happened, then consider praying again for that person; if you do, involve the whole group in the prayer. But remember that sometimes the Holy Spirit comes and there is no immediate evidence of his presence. A good example of this is the evangelist Billy Graham. At first he experienced nothing tangible, and it was only later that it became evident that the power of God had come upon him in a big way.

End by listening again to the song 'This is the air I breathe'. Would they like to sing it?

Beyond Ourselves

Session 9 : God's promises

Things you will need for this session :

- A whiteboard or flipchart
- Bibles
- A large piece of paper or card with 2 Peter 1.4 written out
- Small cards on which group members can write the key verse.
- Perhaps a stole for you to wear as you play the part of a minister.

Faithfulness and trust   (15 mins)

Open in prayer. Thank God for the gift of the Spirit and ask that the Spirit's presence may be felt in the group as you meet today.

Explain that today's session will be all about promises, and that to illustrate you will begin by thinking about the promises people make when they get married. Ask for two volunteers to play the parts of bride and groom on their wedding day. If there is a married couple in the group, choose them.

Tell the volunteers that their names are Tom and Mary, and ask them to stand facing each other. You, as leader, will play the part of the priest or minister. As in a real wedding, you will feed the lines to them and they will repeat them, first Tom and then Mary. Stand with Tom and Mary as they say the vows. If those playing Tom and Mary are not actually married, ask them to feel the seriousness of the vows even though they are only acting.

Read the vows, pausing at each / in the text below, and ask first Tom and then Mary to repeat them after you:

"I, Tom/ take you Mary/ to be my wife/for better for worse/for richer for poorer/ in sickness and in health/ to love and to cherish/ till death us do part./With my body I honour you/All that I am I give to you/All that I have I share with you/ This is my solemn promise."

"I, Mary" etc.

Explain to the group that once these promises have been made, it is your job as priest or minister to join their hands and pronounce them man and wife. If the actors playing Tom and Mary are a couple, do that now.

Ask Tom and Mary to sit down and then ask who in the group has ever made those, or similar, promises? Some may have made the promises in a church, others in a secular setting, others in private with no-one else present. However it was done ask them how they felt about it at the time?

Now ask the group what can go wrong? At the beginning these promises are sincerely made. But sometimes it doesn't work out. Why is this? Why do relationships that have a good beginning sometimes fail?

Allow them to answer, and draw out these two things:

- Sometimes there is a lack of faithfulness. Tom, or Mary, or both, make solemn promises but they do not keep them. This can be because the promises, made at a time when emotions were strong, were never properly thought through.

- Sometimes there is a lack of trust. Mary tries her best to keep the promises but Tom fails to trust her intentions. Every time Mary fails to get it quite right Tom suspects her motives.

Ask the group what other human relationships they have which depend on faithfulness and trust? The answer is that all lasting relationships have to be based on these two principles.

Explain that our relationship with God is also based on promises, some which he makes and some which we make. So our relationship with God also depends on faithfulness and trust. We have to make up our minds to be faithful in keeping our vows to God. We also have to make up our minds to maintain our trust in what God has promised to us.

Our promises to God   (15 mins)

Give each member of the group a piece of paper and ask them to write out in their own words what it is that they believe themselves to have promised to God. Give them a few minutes to write, and then a few minutes to share in twos or threes what they have written.

Interrupt the discussion and refer them to the prayer of commitment on page 40 of the coursebooks. Say that some of us have said this prayer or something similar. If we said this prayer we actually made five promises.

- We promised to trust Jesus about the past
- We promised to trust Jesus about the future
- We promised to live by his priorities
- We promised to be unashamed of him
- We promised that we will try our best not to do anything that is wrong

Ask the group to sit in silence for a moment, to read through the prayer carefully and to contemplate the seriousness of the promises they have made, or perhaps in some cases have yet to make.

God's promises to us   (30 mins)

Having looked briefly at the promises we have made to God, move on to look at the promises God has made to us.

Keeping people in twos and threes, refer each group to page 59 in their coursebooks, where they will find three Bible passages, **Psalm 103.10-12, 1 Peter 3.18, 1 John 1.7-9**.

Ask the group to look at the passages and answer two questions:

- What, in a nutshell, is the promise that God has made to us?

- Some people trust in this promise. Others do not. How will this trust or lack of it show in the way these two groups of people live?

Give them 8 minutes and then interrupt. At this stage do not ask for their answers but instead ask them to look at two further passages, **John 10.27-29** and **Romans 8.31-39**.

As before ask the groups to look at the passages and answer the same two questions: what is the promise, and what difference will trusting it make to our lives?

After a further 8 minutes give them two more passages, but this time explain the contexts. In **John 14.1-6** Jesus is facing death and the disciples are frightened; the passage tells us what Jesus said to reassure them. In **Philippians 1.20-23** Paul is writing from prison and he too is facing the likelihood of imminent execution.

Ask the groups to look at the two passages and answer the same questions as before: what is the promise, and what difference will it make if we believe it?

After a further 8 minutes bring them together and ask them what the promise was in each case. Summarise their answers as follows:

- The first promise is about the past – whatever we have done in the past God promises to forgive and forget

- The second promise is for the present – nothing can separate us from the love of God

- The third promise is about the future – when I die I will be given a new life in the presence of God.

Considering these three promises one at a time, ask the group what kind of behaviour on our part would show that we really do trust in these promises. The kind of answers you are looking for are as follows:

If we trust in the first promise

- We will not allow ourselves to carry around a load of guilt for our past mistakes but will forgive ourselves as God has forgiven us.
- When we sin we will be quick to confess our sins and receive God's forgiveness.
- We will then resolve to do better in future and we will ask God to help us.
- Because we know that we have been forgiven we will easily forgive others.

If we trust in the second promise

- We will approach each day joyfully confident that we will see many signs of God's loving hand on our lives
- We will be quick to bring our needs to God and ask for his help
- When danger looms we will not be afraid
- When things go wrong we will maintain our confidence in God and continue to praise him. We will say 'God knows me – God loves me – God has a plan – I will trust him.'

If we trust in the third promise

- We will not fear death
- We will live every day to the full
- We will often set our minds on the things that are to come
- We will love to worship God because we know that in eternity worship will be our greatest joy

Ask the group to pause for a moment, to close their eyes and pray silently. Is there anything about the way they are living which needs to change and be replaced by a quiet trust in God?

God's promise comes with a guarantee   (15 mins)

Explain that God's promises are much easier to believe than human promises because God's promises come with a guarantee. Ask if they can remember the guarantee which confirms the truth of God's promises. The guarantee is the gift of the Holy Spirit. Because we have the Holy Spirit in our lives, we know that the promises which we have listed on the board are true. The past is forgiven. God's love surrounds us every day. Our future is with God in heaven.

Remind them that last week you prayed together that the Holy Spirit would be given to each member of the group. Ask them what their experience has been since then? Refer them to page 61 of the coursebooks where they will find the following list:

Early signs of the Holy Spirit's presence in our lives:

- a new peace
- a new happiness
- a new awareness of when we are doing wrong
- a special love for other Christians
- a new desire to do good
- answers to prayers
- a desire to tell others about Jesus
- finding that the Bible is speaking to us, especially the verses we are learning,

Have they experienced any of these things during the last few weeks?

Ask if any of the group has a close relationship with someone who really loves them. This might be a husband or wife, a mother or father, or just a friend. If so, ask them how they know that this person loves them.

Let them answer but then say that although love is occasionally shown by big things, for example an act of great sacrifice or a very expensive present, day to day love is shown mostly by small things such as a touch or a smile or a kind word.

Then say that the list on page 61 in the coursebooks is a list of the little things that the Spirit does for us every day to let us know that he is there and loves us. The fact that we are experiencing these little things is the guarantee that the big promises are true and will be kept. Our sins **are** forgiven, God's love **does** surround us, we **are** going to live on with God after we die.

Key verse   (10 mins)

Ask for several volunteers to recite the eight key verses you have learned so far.

Then introduce the key verse for this week and learn it together.

2 Peter 1.4: 'Thus he has given us, through these things, his precious and very great promises, so that through them you may escape from the corruption that is in the world because of lust, and may become participants in the divine nature.'

Hand out blank cards for group members to write out the verse and put it in their wallet or purse.

A time of prayer   (5 mins)

Say to the group that you will end the session today with a time of prayer thanking God for the promises he has given. You will also reaffirm the promises which you have made to him.

The prayer is printed in the coursebooks on page 61 and is also printed here. Give the group a moment to read through the prayer quietly and then suggest that together you offer up this prayer to God. Ask different group members to read out the paragraphs of the prayer:

"Father God, we speak to you today to affirm our trust in the promises which you have made to us. First, we thank you Father that, because Jesus has died for us on the cross, we can be sure that all our sins have been forgiven and forgotten by you. We promise to forgive ourselves, to forget about the past, and to move on with our lives, looking forward to what you have planned for us.

"Father, we thank you for your promise that nothing can ever separate us from your love. Thank you that through our faith in Jesus we have come into your family. We are now your children and, through the presence of the Holy Spirit in our lives, we experience your love every day. We promise that we will expect good things from you and that when they come we will acknowledge you and thank you.

"Father, we thank you that even when hard things happen in our lives your love still surrounds us. We thank you that you know us, you love us, and that you always have a plan. We promise that whatever happens we will trust you and continue to praise you.

"Father, we thank you for your promise of eternal life. We promise to think often about the great reward that is ahead of us. We thank you that Jesus was faithful to you even to the point of death and that he now reigns with you in glory. We thank you that Jesus promised that what happened to him will also happen to us and we promise that as he was faithful so will we be.

"Father, we thank you that Jesus made it completely clear how his disciples were to live. We have decided to be his disciples and to live by his priorities. We promise to study his teaching carefully and to apply it diligently to our lives.

"Father, we want to tell you that we have turned our backs on sin. If you show us that something is wrong we are resolved not to do it. When we find that temptation is strong, or that we are weak, we will always seek your help. We want to be those who overcome and not those who are defeated.

"Father, our loyalty to Jesus is absolute. We love him, we worship him. He is our God as you are our God. We will always honour him and always hope to speak of him to others. It will be our greatest delight and dearest hope to lead others to believe in him and to know him for themselves."

Beyond Ourselves

Session 10 : Living by faith

Things you will need for this session :

- A whiteboard or flipchart
- Bibles
- A large piece of paper or card with **Hebrews 11.6** written out
- Small cards on which group members can write out the key verse
- A large card with the promises on page 103 written up
- A few tea lights
- A bowl of water
- a piece of paper and a pen for each person

Faith in God's promises   (20 mins)

Open in prayer. Thank God for his promises. Thank him for his forgiveness, for the fact that his love surrounds us, and for the promise of eternal life. Thank him for the gift of the Spirit who guarantees all of God's promises.

Remind the group that our relationship with God is based on promises – promises made by us to God and promises made by God to us.

Prepare the following summary in advance, put it up in a prominent place, and talk the group through it. Allow time for them to ask questions. It is important that they understand clearly what the promises are.

MY PROMISES TO GOD

I will trust in God's forgiveness, in his unending care, and in his promise of eternal life.

I will try my best to live by the teaching and example of Jesus, depending on the Holy Spirit to help me.

I will be unashamed of Jesus before others and will serve him in everything I do.

GOD'S PROMISES TO ME

All my past sins and failures are forgiven and forgotten, dealt with on the cross.

I have become a permanent member of God's family. God is now my Father, and no matter what happens to me he will always love me and never abandon me.

This will continue forever – when I die I will live again in the presence of God.

During this life the Holy Spirit, who I received when I first believed, will never be taken from me.

Remind them now that when two people get married they make vows, and the bargain is clear. Each of them has said "I will always be faithful to you", and each has said "I will always trust you" – and each means it. For a while things go well. Promises are kept. Trust is maintained. But then something goes wrong. Promises are not kept, or trust is not maintained, or both. This is a moment of crisis. Usually the issue is faced. Apologies are made. Forgiveness is sought and given. And the couple begin again. This continues until the next moment of crisis. And so on. This is how a normal healthy marriage works.

It is also how a normal healthy relationship with God works. Everything is fine until either we are unfaithful to God or we fail to trust him. When this happens there is a moment of crisis in our spiritual journey. Usually these crises get resolved easily and all is well again. But occasionally the crisis does not get resolved and people spend months or years in a spiritual desert.

Unfaithfulness   (30 mins)

Say that this session will be about how to handle these occasional crises in our relationship with God. If we know what to do, this should avoid us ever having any big problems. So you are going to think together first about unfaithfulness and then about lack of trust.

Turn together to **Lamentations 3.22-23**. There is no question of God being unfaithful. Tell the group some stories of your own experience of God's faithfulness and invite them to share some of theirs.

On the board you have listed four of God's great promises. God has many other promises for us than these four. To illustrate, look with the group at **John 15.7, John 14.27** and **James 1.5**. From these verses we see that God promises to answer prayers, he promises to give us his peace, and he promises to provide us with wisdom. God will keep these promises too – as he keeps all his promises.

God is always faithful to us but what about us – are we faithful to him? Turn with the group to **Romans 7.15**. They will see that the apostle Paul was full of good intentions – he meant to be faithful – but to his dismay he did not always live up to his intentions. Paul had lapses. Every Christian has lapses.

Reinforce to them that failure is a normal part of the Christian experience. Since you last met have they caught themselves swearing, letting someone down, telling a lie, having too much to drink? If they did it's is not a disaster, but it is something that needs dealing with. Divide the group into threes, and ask them to focus on the three promises which they have all made to God and which are listed on your board: we have promised to trust, we have promised to follow, and we have promised to be unashamed.

Ask them to share with each other any ways in which they have failed to live up to these promises. Do they sometimes feel as Paul felt – "If only I could get this right?" Say that it is good to trust each other and admit our failures to each other, but that if anyone feels embarrassed they should feel comfortable not to share.

After a few minutes bring the group together again and say that whenever we are confronted by our own unfaithfulness there are two things to do and one thing not to do – two do's and one don't.

1. Don't listen to Satan

Say that you will start with the 'don't'. **Don't** listen to the accusing voice of Satan, who will say to you that you are a failure, that God does not love you anymore, and that it is time for you to give up being a Christian. Has anyone has heard that voice? Be prepared to share your own experience.

Ask, "What is it that is able to separate us from the love of God?". The answer of course is 'nothing'. Explain that this means that a few mistakes on our part do not mean that God has stopped loving us. Look together at **2 Timothy 2.13**.

If anyone in the group appears to be really struggling with their failures ask if you may pray for them. In your prayer assert the fact that nothing can separate this person from God's love and also assert our authority over Satan.

2. Confess your failings to God

Then say that the first 'do' is to confess the matter to God and ask for his forgiveness. Turn with the group to **1 John 1.9** and ask what will happen if we do this.

The answer is that we will be forgiven and will be given help to avoid making the same mistake again. Why will we be forgiven? Why will we be helped? The answer is in the verse. We are forgiven and helped because God is faithful. No matter how many times we are unfaithful, if we confess our sins to God, he will forgive us, help us and cleanse us.

If you need to reinforce the promise you could look also at **Proverbs 28.13** and **Hebrews 10.17**.

Then give each person a piece of paper and ask them to write down any way in which they feel they have failed God. At the top of the paper they should write 'My confession'. Say that if there is nothing to write that is fine – you don't want them to make things up!

While they are writing prepare some tea lights and a bowl of water. Then suggest to each member of the group that when they have written out their confessions they should set their piece of paper alight and then dowse it in water. This is a picture of our past failures being forgiven and forgotten – burned up and gone, consigned to the past and having no influence on the future.

3. Set your mind on spiritual things

The second 'do' is to do what Paul did. We saw in **Romans 7.15** that sometimes Paul was struggling, apparently unable to live up to the standards he had set for himself. Look now at **Romans 8.5** where Paul says what he did about it. Paul writes that he 'set his mind on the things of the Spirit.' Whenever he did that he found that he was able to gain victory over himself. The Holy Spirit within him was stronger than his moral weakness (what Paul called his 'flesh').

Ask the group how they think they could set their minds on the things of the Spirit. Let them answer and acknowledge that there are many ways. But explain that if a Christian sets his mind on a sordid film or even on the newspapers, or if he sets his mind to worry about something, this will quickly affect the way that he thinks and behaves.

But if a Christian sets his mind on God, on how wonderful he is, on the things which God is doing or saying, then he will soon find that his life, the things which he himself says and does, will be transformed.

Here are some good ways to set our minds on things of the Spirit. This list can be found in the coursebooks on page 69.

- Enjoying creation, the things which God has made
- Meditating on the key verses that have been part of this course
- Having a time of quiet in the morning for reflection and prayer
- Going to church
- Coming to the group meeting
- Singing hymns and spiritual songs
- Reading the Bible
- Listening to CDs of sermons or spiritual music
- Listening to the Spirit and being obedient to his voice
- Any of the things listed in **Philippians 4.8**

Talk through this list, inviting people to share ways in which they have been blessed as they have devoted time to these things, and sharing your own experiences too.

Ask the group to sit quietly, and to choose one of the key verses which we have been using on the course. As a way of setting their minds on the things of the Spirit ask them each to spend some time in meditation on the verse they have chosen. After a while ask each to share one positive thought from that verse. After the meditation and before the sharing listen to (or sing) the song 'This is the air I breathe' (the words are on page 53 in the coursebooks).

Key verse

Next move the group on from thinking about unfaithfulness and concentrate on the other problem , lack of trust. Say that another word for trust is faith. All Christians have crises of faith but how are these to be handled? Begin by turning to the key verse for this week, **Hebrews 11.6**:

'And without faith it is impossible to please God, for whoever would approach him must believe that he exists and that he rewards those who seek him.'

Learn the verse together, then hand out cards for people to write it out.

Doubts (25 mins)

Ask the group to look again at the four promises which you have listed under the heading 'God's promises to me.' And remind them of the other promises which you looked at earlier when you saw that God promises to answers prayers (**John 15.7**), he promises to grant peace (**John 14.27**), and he promises to provide wisdom (**James 1.5**).

The key verse, **Hebrews 11.6**, says that the way to please God is to maintain our trust in all these promises. As we please God by trusting him we find that God will reward us. This sounds easy but it often is not. Faith can easily slip away. Warn the group that every Christian has doubts – not all the time but sometimes.

Divide the group into threes and ask them to share any doubts that they have been having, and what they think the reasons are for these doubts. Say that very likely some of them will have been having no doubts at all, in which case they should say so and then listen to the others.

Bring the group together again and then ask them what they think it is that causes us to doubt. In the discussion that follows make sure you cover the following points:

- **We doubt because of things that happen in our lives**

   For example we do something wrong and are ashamed of ourselves, and we say to ourselves 'How could God possibly forgive me?' This is us doubting the first promise.

When something goes badly wrong for us, we say 'Does God really love me?' Now we are doubting the second promise.

Perhaps someone close to us dies, and we say 'Is there really life after death?' Now we are doubting the third promise.

We neglect prayer, worship, and Bible study. We are failing to give attention to the things of the Spirit so our spiritual lives run dry. Because we are out of touch with God's power we begin to doubt if it is real. We are doubting the fourth promise.

We pray and there is no answer. We are afraid and can't find peace. We are confused and can't find a way forward. All these things can cause us to doubt God and his love for us.

- **We doubt because sometimes our feelings deliver negative messages**

  There is undoubtedly a connection between faith and feelings, so if we feel bad it somehow becomes more difficult to have faith. There are many reasons why we may feel bad; for example we become ill, or someone makes an unkind comment, or we get tired, or we overwork or the weather is oppressive. When we feel unhappy, tense or grumpy it is easy to wonder if God is really there because our negative feelings are blocking him from our lives.

- **We doubt because we live in a culture of doubt**

  Everyone doubts, and it rubs off on us. We often hear arguments which are directed against faith in God, and they can be quite persuasive. Some argue, sometimes very effectively, that there is no such thing as God. For a while we find ourselves half-persuaded by these arguments.

Now explain that you have four suggestions for dealing with doubts:

1. Deal with your negative emotions

One cause of doubts is the presence in our lives of negative emotions. The solution is to discover the reason why we are feeling so bad and then try to deal with it. Perhaps you are feeling bad because you have been overworking and are tired or stressed. The solution is to take some time off. Or for example you may be feeling bad because someone has said something unkind or unfair. The solution is to recognise what has happened and then to forgive that person.

Ask if anyone in the group is feeling bad at the moment. If so, try with the group to identify the reason and, once you know what it is, to work out a solution. Then pray together for that person. In particular pray that their faith in God can again become strong.

2. Deal with the negative arguments

Sometimes, often because of circumstances but also because of arguments that are advanced against faith in God, we can find ourselves wondering if God exists at all, or thinking that if he does exist he does not care. When these thoughts come, we should recognise them as being placed in our minds by our spiritual enemy Satan, and deal with them by praying. Turn to **John 8.44**. The things that Jesus taught are true. To disbelieve them is to believe a lie. Satan is the father of lies and all lies come from him. This makes the issue of doubt an issue of spiritual warfare and therefore of prayer.

Before you pray, remind yourself why it is more reasonable to have faith than not to have faith.

Look in turn now at the four promises which God has made to us, and which you listed on your board. Invite people to say why they think each of these promises is true. Let them answer, but bear in mind that it always boils down to three things:

1. We believe because we believe the testimony of the Bible about Jesus.

2. We believe because we accept the testimony of Christians, throughout history but especially today, that these things are true in their lives. We are not in this alone; we are part of a believing community.

3. We believe because of our own past experience of God's faithfulness.

These are strong and persuasive reasons for believing in God's promises. No one can provide scientific proof of the reliability of God's promises, but the evidence is very strong.

3. Pray away your doubts

Return to the key verse **Hebrews 11.6**. We have seen that faith is more reasonable than doubt, but that faith is not proof. The only way to make progress is to make a firm decision that you will trust God.

Ask the group to turn to page 69 in the coursebooks where they will find a prayer; ask them to join with you in saying it. Allow them to read the prayer first and then say it together out loud. The prayer is as follows:

'Father, we admit that sometimes we doubt you. We doubt that you exist. We doubt that you love us. We doubt that you have forgiven us. We doubt that you will answer our prayers. We doubt the promise of eternal life.

'Father, we are sorry that we sometimes doubt you. We are like Thomas who doubted even though all the evidence was there for him to believe. We thank you Jesus for the gracious way you dealt with Thomas, and we ask you to be gracious to us.

'We acknowledge that these doubts originate in our spiritual enemy Satan. In the name of Jesus we cut ourselves off from him and claim your protection. As Jesus prayed, so we pray 'Father, keep us from the evil one.'

'Father, we know that we can only please you if we will believe in you. So we commit ourselves once again to being believers, people who will put our trust in you and wait for you to respond. We look for you to reward us once again by giving us your Spirit.'

4. Set your minds on the things of the Spirit

We have been having doubts and finding it hard to trust God. So what do we do? Explain that we should start by examining our negative feelings and the factors that have been causing them. Perhaps this is not a problem about doubt, but about tiredness or stress at work or another factor. Then we should remind ourselves of the reason why it is logical to have faith in God. Then we should pray, acknowledging that our spiritual enemy Satan is actively trying to get us to doubt, and committing ourselves once again to being believers.

Then finally, to deal with our doubts we must set our minds on the things of the Spirit.

Look again at page 69 in the coursebooks, and remind the group of some of the ways in which we can do this. If we do these things, we shall find that the Spirit is once again active in our lives. Look too at page 61 in the coursebooks and reread the list of the things that the Spirit loves to do for us. These are the rewards promised in **Hebrews 11.6**. Reassure them that once these things begin to happen then we find that our doubts will go away.

Writing a prayer (15 mins)

Give each person in the group pen and paper. Ask them to write a prayer in the first person, thanking God for what he has done and perhaps also for what they have learned during this course. When everyone has finished, pray together as a group, inviting each person to read out what they have written.

There may still be some in the group who were not ready to say either of the commitment prayers which came in sessions 6 and 8. If so, notice carefully how they have handled this final prayer exercise. If you now feel that they may be ready to commit themselves to God, suggest that they say a further prayer and that the group pray for them to receive the Spirit.

Looking ahead to Book 2 (5 mins)

The course is now complete! Thank them for their faithfulness in coming, and for their friendship.

Tell them that what happens next will be very important for all of them. Urge them to continue to belong to a similar group, because this is the best way to learn and to get to know more of God. Make sure they understand that the Christian life was never intended to be something that we do on our own, but something that we do with other people.

Every context will be different and you may have other plans, not just for the group but for yourself as well. But be aware that if Book 1 has gone well, an excellent way forward for the group would be to continue with Book 2, which is called *The New Community*. If this is what you would like to do, suggest it to the group and make sure you have some copies of the Member's Coursebooks to show them.

Key verses

Psalm 23.6 – 'Surely goodness and mercy shall follow me all the days of my life, and I shall dwell in the house of the LORD my whole life long.'

Romans 6.23 – 'For the wages of sin is death, but the free gift of God is eternal life in Christ Jesus our Lord.'

John 1:12 – 'But to all who received him, who believed in his name, he gave power to become children of God.'

John 3.16 – 'For God so loved the world that he gave his only Son, so that everyone who believes in him may not perish but may have eternal life.'

1 Peter 3.18 – 'For Christ also suffered for sins once for all, the righteous for the unrighteous, in order to bring you to God. He was put to death in the flesh, but made alive in the spirit.'

Acts 2.38 – 'Peter said to them, 'Repent, and be baptized every one of you in the name of Jesus Christ so that your sins may be forgiven; and you will receive the gift of the Holy Spirit.'

Luke 11.13 – 'If you then, who are evil, know how to give good gifts to your children, how much more will the heavenly Father give the Holy Spirit to those who ask him!'

John 7.37-39 – 'Let anyone who is thirsty come to me, and let the one who believes in me drink. As the scripture has said, "Out of the believer's heart shall flow rivers of living water." 'Now he said this about the Spirit, which believers in him were to receive.'

2 Peter 1.4 – 'He has given us, through these things, his precious and very great promises, so that through them you may escape from the corruption that is in the world because of lust, and may become participants in the divine nature.'

Hebrews 11.6 – 'And without faith it is impossible to please God, for whoever would approach him must believe that he exists and that he rewards those who seek him.'

Other Publications from The Mathetes Trust

Beyond Ourselves is the first book of *The God Who is There*, a discipleship programme in three parts recommended by the Anglican Communion report *Intentional Discipleship*. We recommend you follow it with:

Book 2: The New Community. This second part of the course is modelled on the discipleship patterns of the New Testament, where we see that being a disciple of Jesus is not an individual but a shared activity. It enables participants to discover what it means to be part of a group of people who are seeking God in and through their relationships with one another. The course includes worship, facilitated through a specially commissioned CD by Phil Lawson Johnston.

Book 3: Shining Like Stars is the third book in *The God Who is There* series. It focusses on what it means to live as effective Christian disciples in the midst of the challenges of daily life, and its aim is to equip people to live with compassion and integrity as Christians in the community and in the workplace. The course includes worship.

We publish a range of other books, booklets and course materials. Some of those which may interest you include:

Following Jesus: The Plural of Disciple is Church, by Alison Morgan

"God has already used Alison Morgan's inspired writing to touch very many lives. This wonderful new book addresses the question of discipleship, a crucial one for today's church. She insightfully and engagingly elucidates what it means to be a disciple of Jesus and rightly insists that only as disciples together, as church, shall we be a truly effective part of God's great mission to transform not just individuals but the whole creation in Christ."
John Inge, Bishop of Worcester

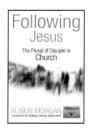

115

Courses to support evangelism and discipleship

Beautiful Lives is a group course by Roger Morgan which helps church members develop the confidence to share their faith naturally and effectively with friends, family, colleagues and neighbours.

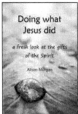

Doing what Jesus did - a fresh look at the gifts of the Spirit by Alison Morgan is a welcome, readable and original introduction to a key topic about which little has been written in recent years. It includes a group study.

In His Name - a training course for healing prayer teams, by Alison Morgan and John Woolmer, is a tried and tested 8 session course to train those appointed to pray with others in or on behalf of the local church.

Season of renewal, a Lent course by Alison Morgan and Bill Goodman, combines traditional elements with a fresh approach, and is ideal for groups who want something a little different which will act as a stimulus for future growth.

For more information or to find out how we can support you in the use of these materials please visit https://mathetestrust.org or contact us at admin@mathetestrust.org.